THE YEAR OF THE OATH

A Da Capo Press Reprint Series

CIVIL LIBERTIES IN AMERICAN HISTORY

GENERAL EDITOR: LEONARD W. LEVY

Claremont Graduate School

THE YEAR OF THE OATH

The Fight for Academic Freedom
at the University of California

BY GEORGE R. STEWART

in collaboration with other professors

of the University of California

DA CAPO PRESS • NEW YORK • 1971

THE YEAR OF THE OATH

THE YEAR OF THE OATH

The Fight for Academic Freedom
at the University of California

BY GEORGE R. STEWART

in collaboration with other professors
of the University of California

DOUBLEDAY & COMPANY, INC.

Garden City, New York, 1950

CONTENTS

Part One: Introduction and History

    1. The Year of the Oath, 9
    2. On Freedom and Tenure, 14
    3. The Issues, 20
    4. The History of the Controversy:
       A Calendar, 27
    5. The T.A. and the Piano Player, 41
    6. Power Drive against the University, 49

Part Two: Results

    7. The Damage, 58
    8. Life in the Ivory Tower, 65

Part Three: Larger Aspects

    9. "You too can have a loyalty oath!" 82
    10. "This is the way it begins." 90

Part Four: The Regential System

    11. Memory Book, 99

5

12. Do the Regents Represent the People? 108
13. To the Dissident Minority: A Letter, 117

Part Five: Conclusion

14. What Should We Do About It? 123
15. Unfinished Business, 131

Postscript, 138

Appendix A: Documents, 145

Appendix B: Roster, 152

Authors' Note and Sources, 154

THE YEAR OF THE OATH

Part One: Introduction and History

The Year of the Oath

That was the Year of the Oath. It was neither a calendar year nor an academic year. It ran from just before examinations to just before examinations, and straddled across from 1949 to 1950.

In that year we went to oath meetings, and talked oath, and thought oath. We woke up, and there was the oath with us in the delusive bright cheeriness of the morning. "Oath" read the headline in the newspaper, and it put a bitter taste into the breakfast coffee. We discussed the oath during lunch at the Faculty Club. And what else was there for subject matter at the dinner table? Then we went to bed, and the oath hovered over us in the darkness, settling down as a nightmare of wakefulness.

Then, in the hours of the night, Academic Freedom and all the other high ideals drew far off and seemed small, and each man or woman, alone, faced "Sign-or-get-out!" in terms of next month's bills, or the daughter to be kept in college, or the payments on the house and the baby due in the summer, or the ever-recurrent thought, "At my age, could I get another job?"

There were the ups and downs. June and July were bad; August was quieter; September was tense. The Christmas vacation, for most of us, was fortunately a calm interlude. But after each lull the crisis built up more fiercely than before.

Many of us, one would guess, aged more than one year during that time. Toward the end, when we thought back, more than twelve months seemed to have passed since Edward rose in the meeting and said he would not sign. There were some moments of exaltation during that year, as when the chorus of ayes came solidly from the massed Senate like the shout of a cheering host, or when we in Berkeley heard that Los Angeles, too, was standing fast. There were more moments of bitterness, and of doubt and suspicion and dread.

We sent our leaders in to fight for us. Though we are a large faculty, these were men we knew and trusted. Ben and Joel tried first, then Malcolm, then John. One after the other they came back beaten or compromising, and at times we ourselves lost confidence in them, and some of us reviled them. Now we see, or should see, that things of that sort were bound to happen during the Year of the Oath, when strain and uncertainty preyed upon our minds.

Yes, we remember, too, when one of our leaders collapsed in the Senate meeting, having worked harder than a man should and taken more than a man ought.

We came to realize why they always came back beaten. They were bare-handed men going in to fight against the men who held the guns. (What had saved us at all was that we had some friends among those who held the guns.) Other phrases, other images came to our minds and were familiar to us during that year—the knife at the throat—fighting on the edge of a precipice.

We learned a good deal. We learned something about standing together and fighting in close order, although professors are individualists and not naturally good at that. Perhaps we grew wiser during the year; some of us grew more cynical. We learned also something about how suspicion arises, and mistrust, and fear. Of men whom we had known for twenty years we heard it said, "You can't be sure of him!" Before then these were only things we had read about in books as having happened years ago or in other countries.

The long strain wore us down. We made mistakes. We did things we were later to regret. At times we were not as idealistic or as courageous as we should have been. Blame us if you like.

Yes, it was the month-after-month strain that wore us down, and the sense that we were always on the defensive, with nothing to win except what we had possessed at the beginning, though that indeed was something very fine in human life. We were trying to hold the lines, plug a gap here, and stop a hole there. We had none of that high exhilaration that comes with the advance toward victory.

Out of this feeling sprang the idea of this book. To some of us came the realization that the strength of the opposing group of regents was not really omnipotent, that their position was actually weak.

California, and our campus, was never more beautiful than in that spring, when March ran into April. But to the shame of our state and of our University it must be said that we felt it necessary to organize for the writing of this book as the French organized their *Résistance* during the years of the Nazis, with radiating lines of responsibility and with no one knowing all the others who were involved. At that time sober and serious professors flatly refused to talk over the University telephone line on such a matter as this. Men, on being asked to help, calmly asked, "What is the risk?" and then generally went ahead in any case. Whether all these precautions were necessary may now be argued, and will certainly be doubted by those who were not there. But it cannot be argued that this state of mind did not exist, and when such a state of mind has been produced in a faculty of university professors, that condition is in itself a doleful actuality.

Although the original intention was to publish anonymously, more mature consideration yielded the decision that the book would be more authoritative if signed. The names of the other workers are still withheld and are indeed not recorded anywhere nor all known to any one person. The editorial *we* is, however, used freely and represents a reality, not a convention.

Finally, on April 21, 1950, the regents withdrew the requirement of the special oath and modified the flat "Sign-or-get-out!" We thus escaped, temporarily at least, the worst disaster, although our situation still remained tense and even as of the date of going to press (June 4) continues uncertain.

In this book, therefore, we join our forces with those ten regents, including the governor of the state and the president of the University, who on March 31, 1950, voted for the rescinding of the special oath without qualification. Our approach is positive rather than negative. Our objectives are three.

First, in so far as space permits, we present the factual record. The research has been done by highly trained scholars and the result is, we are confident, so professional that the book will undoubtedly be a permanent work of reference.

Second, the attempt has been made to interpret these facts, not only as they relate to the University of California and the state, but also as they relate to all our universities and to the nation. Not only, we believe, is this University threatened, along with the others, but also there is a threat to many of the traditional ways of American democracy.

Third, positive proposals for long-range improvement are put forward, particularly in that important chapter, "What Should We Do About It?"

Having been written by members of the faculty, the book necessarily represents a faculty point of view. At the present time any full collaboration with the regents is impossible, and since a Standing Order of the regents forbids the direct approach of a professor to a regent, we have not sought counsel even from our friends. On the other hand, this book cannot be said always to represent *the* faculty point of view, for except in such large matters as general opposition to the oath, the faculty was not well enough unified to have a single opinion. In the final analysis the point of view may be considered that of the signatory author, although he has deferred to his collaborators, frequently as to fact, and sometimes as to interpretation. Among the collaborators many differences of opinion existed, but all agreed upon the general objectives, and in the preparation of the book no argument arose.

The book deals primarily with the controversy as it has concerned the regents and the Academic Senate. At the University of California the Academic Senate consists of professors, including associate and assistant professors, and instructors. Other parts of the complex University body— non-Senate academic employees, administration, students, alumni, non-academic employees—have also been seriously affected. In particular, the non-Senate academic employees (NSAE), consisting chiefly of lecturers, teaching assistants, and research associates, have waged a fight more vigorous in some respects even than that of the Senate. The president of the University has also been very deeply involved. Nevertheless, although recognizing these ramifications, we have largely omitted them from consideration because of limitations of space and in the interests of simplicity.

A few words are necessary as to the general structure of the University. Operating throughout the state on eight campuses, its professors and instructors are organized into a Senate (Northern Section), meeting at Berkeley, and a Senate (Southern Section), meeting at Los Angeles. The two are independent but take joint action in all matters of University-wide concern. During the period of the controversy the Northern Section happened, according to its schedule, to meet a few days before its sister section, and because of this accident it initiated the greater amount of business. The independence and equality of the two sections should, however, always be remembered.

The present book shows a certain northern tone, having been conceived and written in Berkeley. Members of the Southern Section, however, collaborated and indeed generously abandoned plans of their own in order to throw their strength into a unified volume.

This, then, is a history of the oath controversy, written both with reference to the University of California and to the nation as a whole, not only for members of university faculties, but also for the general public. It is not without concrete incident and drama, but it can best begin with a brief consideration of two abstractions, the meaning of which must be grasped before the significance of the whole controversy can be understood.

CHAPTER 2

On Freedom and Tenure

On April 22, 1950, the San Francisco *Chronicle* presented a front-page editorial under the title "Oath Controversy." From it we quote:

It's hard . . . even for an articulate scholar to make academic freedom and the principle of tenure crystal clear to the layman.

Hard it may be, just as the explanation of anything else essentially simple is likely to be hard. Since this book, however, is being written for the unprofessional public, we must try to make these matters clear, the more especially since, by making them clear, we also can scarcely fail to demonstrate their importance.

By Academic Freedom is meant merely—*the freedom, within an educational institution, to teach and to be taught the truth*. It is as simple as that, and as important.

The proviso, "within an educational institution," is necessary to distinguish Academic Freedom, of particular application to teachers, from Freedom of Speech, which is a right of all people in a democracy, teachers included. The constitutional principle of Freedom of Speech, in which anyone (including a professor) should be protected by the police, keeps a man from being jailed if he speaks an unpopular truth. The principle of Academic Freedom, in which a teacher should be protected by the governing body (regents or other) of his institution, keeps him from losing his job if he teaches an unpopular truth.

Lest there should be any lack of crystal clarity, let us look back at the words of our definition to see if they should be further explained. *Freedom* and *truth,* though vague and difficult words, are here used in no special sense and should be generally intelligible. Who shall determine what is truth and what not truth is always a difficult problem, but the strong public trust in universities rests upon the belief that a faculty is composed of specialists in such determination.

The word *teach* must, of course, be taken in a large sense, to include not only ordinary teaching but also publication. Certainly, in publishing the results of his research, the professor merely becomes teacher to the world, and his freedom to that end must certainly be maintained.

The distinction between the active verb (*teach*) and the passive (*to be taught*) calls for comment, since it brings out a generally neglected point.

Too often discussions of Academic Freedom assume that the teacher is the most vitally concerned party. This is incorrect. The teacher, even if his institution restricts Academic Freedom, can still hold his job by accepting the slur against his professional pride and the impairment of his human integrity. Though he may be restrained from teaching the truth, he knows what it is and that it exists. The student is worse o.ſ. In an institution that restricts Academic Freedom his education will be stunted. He may not even be able to learn the truth, or even that it exists at all!

Let us have one anecdote. . . . A writer, having published a popular exposition of Darwinism, received a bewildered letter. "You seem," his correspondent wrote, "to be presenting something about the origin of animals that is different from Genesis. This is very interesting. Is there another theory?" The apparently intelligent and open-minded writer of this letter might have been educated in an institution which restricted Academic Freedom. Not only had he been kept from forming an opinion as to whether Darwinism was true or false, but he did not even know that it existed.

It should be added that Academic Freedom is important also for the whole general public. Our faculties should be both the watchdogs of already established truth and the hounds that continually pursue truth into its most distant hiding places. To restrict their freedom in either of these functions is to endanger the maintenance and the extension of civilization.

As regards Tenure—that is a very common idea and should be correspondingly easy to grasp. Any union man should know what professors mean by Tenure, and one gathers that most of them actually do. Any high-school teacher whose Tenure is protected by law should know what it means; so should civil-service workers and officers in the Armed Forces. Writers and artists might not be expected to know, but they generally do. Even the white-collar worker, in any decent company, though he may be ununionized, feels that there is a kind of agreer̄ ̇ with the company not to fire him without cause.

Tenure, or Academic Tenure, means merely—*the right of a teacher, after he has amply demonstrated his competence and character, to hold his job, unless proved unfit.*

Again we should consider the words of the definition. . . . Whether we should say "the right" or "the privilege" may be argued. In public debate a professor might be more likely to say "right." In private talk with his colleagues h? might say "privilege" and go on to say: "Being a privilege, it calls for special effort and vigilance on our part to maintain our side of the implicit bargain. In return for the privilege of Tenure we must give exceptional service and must keep our house clean."

The phrase "to hold his job" is clear enough. Perhaps, however, we should add that it should not admit an interpretation which would allow pay reduction, demotion, and the assignment of heavy and embarrassing duties as a means of inducing resignation.

The word "proved" is an important one. As used, it puts

the burden of proof upon those trying to press the charge. This is a point upon which all teachers insist. It is in accord with the basic principle of our law that a man is innocent until proved guilty. The university professor, at least, will also insist that the only people capable of proving him unfit are his professional equals. Along with the physician, the lawyer, and the army officer, he will insist that only those who have attained at least equal eminence in the same specialized profession are capable of sitting in court to judge his professional skill, or integrity, or his character.

The term "unfit" also calls for comment, having two divisions. The conviction for a felony or the commission of various acts considered debasing to the profession is generally considered to prove a professor unfit. He should not, for instance, appear even slightly alcoholic very often, and he should not take his clothes off in the public square even once. As for professional incompetence, that is a more difficult matter. A professor, however, may have to be dismissed —or, more humanely, retired—because of physical debility, or premature senility, or because of mental quirks which pass the professor's ancient prerogative to be a funny old duffer, or because he may become an incompetent drag upon his colleagues, a burden to the university, and a liability to his students. Fortunately, such cases are rare, and with the normal retirement age lowered to sixty-seven, they will be even rarer.

The long clause of the definition, "after he has amply demonstrated his competence and character," is an important qualification. Contrary to much popular belief, a person merely by becoming a member of a university faculty does not attain Tenure. Hence springs the distinction between "tenure staff" and "non-tenure staff" not infrequently heard in discussions about the oath and in any discussion about a university, and likely to be confusing to the layman. In essence, the non-tenure staff consists of the younger men, those still serving their apprenticeship. It is an arduous apprenticeship and a long one. It normally lasts eight years after attainment of a Ph.D. degree. Set by the American Association of

University Professors, this is the standard to which the University of California adheres—unless, indeed, recent events have overthrown this standard along with others.

Full Tenure, and therefore full Academic Freedom, is thus held only by those who have served the University for at least eight years or who by demonstration of unusual ability have attained the rank of associate professor before that time. The non-tenure staff is likely to worry a good deal about lack of Tenure. On the other hand, their theoretical lack of Academic Freedom is generally unimportant. Actually, they stand under the same umbrella with the tenure staff. An outside attempt to infringe upon the freedom of a non-tenure member might, in fact, be very fortunate for him. It would bring his seniors swarming out of the library and the laboratory in his defense, and might make him a symbol to be defended at all costs.

There is also the possibility that the seniors may themselves limit the freedom of the juniors. But I remember only one instance in Berkeley of a non-tenure member so complaining. In his first term he wanted to give a grade of F to a full half of the students in his sections, and some older professors objected. Technically some might think his freedom was infringed, but we are sure that the student body, at least, approved, and the whole matter would be better recorded under the heading of incompetence.

In their practical workings Academic Freedom and Tenure are closely connected. Freedom can hardly exist without Tenure, which relieves the professor of immediate fear. The struggle, therefore, usually rages about Tenure. If he gets Tenure, the professor gets Freedom also. On any campus you will hear ten conversations about Tenure to one about Freedom, for—contrary to belief—many professors are practical men. . . .

We began with the *Chronicle,* and we can also end with it. All who have followed the oath controversy know of that newspaper's magnificent support of the faculty cause. Even in its issue of April 27, 1948, a year before the time of the oath, that newspaper had taken up the defense of Aca-

demic Freedom by publishing a letter, written in 1921, by
Chester Rowell, once editor of the *Chronicle* and a regent for
many years.

Of Academic Freedom he wrote, in terms which would
have seemed fulsome if from a professor's pen:

*I think it is the central liberty of civilization without which
no other liberty could long survive or would be worth keeping.*

As regards interference with that Freedom, he wrote that
pressure by some ordinary citizen might perhaps be tolerated:

*But my voice, as a regent, as of the voice of authority, must
be silent. Such evils, if they exist, must be corrected by
other forces than those of authority.*

CHAPTER 3

The Issues

Between regents and faculty the entire controversy arose from the imposition by the regents of a special oath. In addition to the traditional oath included in the Constitution of the State of California (see Appendix A) and gladly taken already, University employees were suddenly required to swear to a codicil, which in its revised form read:

that I am not a member of the Communist Party, or under any oath, or a party to any agreement, or under any commitment that is in conflict with my obligations under this oath.

The whole controversy, therefore, arose over thirty-four words—or, if the small change of articles, conjunctions, and prepositions be not counted, over about half that number. This is an interesting example of the power over human lives which may be exerted by "mere words," as they are sometimes called. . . .

During the Year of the Oath members of the faculty frequently had to face the question, "Why don't you professors sign?"

This question, of which our businessmen friends seemed particularly fond, was, and remains, difficult to answer. A great many professors had refused to sign and their reasons for refusing were different. Moreover, things changed with the passage of time, so that the reasons for refusing to sign in March were different, to some extent, from those which had loomed large in September or June. Therefore, anyone who seriously thus inquires must not, like Pilate, refuse to stay for an answer, but must, like the wedding guest, sit down and hear the tale to the end. In a sense, this whole book is an answer to the question. . . .

In the first place, however, it must be emphasized that no professor, so far as is known, refused to sign for the obvious reason; that is, that he actually was a Communist. This statement may be made with some confidence for two reasons. First, during the whole heated controversy no one has brought forth evidence to show that any member of the Senate is actually a Communist. Second, if there are any Communists in the Senate, they were probably among the first actually to sign the oath, hoping thus to escape observation, and presumably not being restrained by conscientious scruples against false swearing in the service of the Party.

A certain section of the press has indeed tried consistently to smear the faculty by implying that those who did not sign must be Communists. Moreover, a few regents, apparently to strengthen their own position, seemed to adopt the same attitude, and at least they made no attempt to defend the loyalty of the faculty. Nothing in the whole controversy, in fact, has caused more bitterness among the faculty than this apparent willingness of these regents to allow the reputation of the faculty thus to be gravely injured with the general public.

As to why the professors actually did not sign, some of the reasons may seem to be of small moment in themselves, but these seemingly innocent details represented to the faculty the beginnings of dangerous tendencies—to be combated immediately before they became serious. As one professor put it: "The way to prevent a flood is to keep the first crack from opening in the dam."

The present discussion of the issues is based upon statements collected from various members of the faculty and upon a review of the various resolutions and committee reports. Even with the utmost attempt at simplification, the arguments cannot be reduced to fewer than eight. These are presented to some extent in the order in which they assumed importance during the course of the year. The documents show, however, that the arguments of Tenure and of Academic Freedom were important from the very first and remained so throughout.

1. Ambiguity. In the first arguments, which involved the as-yet-unrevised oath, the charge of ambiguity ranked high. It was pointed out that anyone swearing to such a text would not be certain as to what he was committing himself. After the revision of the text in June, this argument disappeared. It left, however, a heritage of distrust; many believed that the original ambiguity must have sprung from carelessness and must indicate that the regents had voted for the requirement of the oath without much consideration.

2. Political Test. Since the Communist Party is a legal party in California, many professors believed that the oath constituted a political test for membership in the faculty and was therefore contrary, certainly to the spirit, and probably to the letter, of the articles in the state Constitution under which the University operates. They believed also that the establishment of any kind of political test was extremely dangerous. Having been admitted for the Communist Party, it might easily at some later time be extended to include any other party, or any unpopular group. The whole procedure was thus, they believed, contrary to basic American practices and should not be condoned.

3. Guilt by Association. Many professors believed that the blanket condemnation of all members of the Communist Party constituted a recognition of "guilt by association." In other words, people were to be convicted and punished merely because they kept disreputable company, not because they themselves had actually committed any offense or had even been shown likely to commit an offense. They also believed that this was an un-American practice, and a dangerous one, and should be vigorously opposed from its very beginning.

The arguments of political test and guilt by association were extremely strong during the early months of the controversy. Later on, especially after the acceptance of the regents' anti-Communist policy by vote of the faculty, these arguments became of less general importance, although they still remained strongly fixed in many individual minds. If the issue of the oath had been taken to the courts, these arguments would undoubtedly have been again of primary importance.

4. Personal. In the last analysis the very strongest argument with many individuals has been a complex of ideas which may all be placed under the general term "personal." Men and women of spirit objected to having the knife put at their throats; that is, at being forced to swear under penalty of losing their means of livelihood. Moreover, the mere fact of being thus required to swear that you are not a Communist implies that you are under suspicion of being a Communist and is therefore insulting and to be resisted. As others pointed out, the very existence of the second part of the oath implied that a person might have sworn to the traditional oath in bad faith. It was as if, having taken one oath, you then took a second oath to the effect that you had not lied in taking the first one. This might go on forever! To be sure, such procedure was mere foolishness—but then the professor is trained always to resist mere foolishness.

Another strong personal argument was that of discrimination. Why should a particular group of citizens—that is, the professors—be required to swear an oath that is not required of other citizens, not even of state officials? This reduces the professor to a second-class citizen, a person under suspicion. It is comparable to a Jim Crow law. "The time to resist is now!" said some professors, and refused to sign.

5. Not a Good Communist Preventive. Another argument against the oath was that, since Communists would presumably swear to it readily, its imposition was not a practical means of freeing the University from alleged Communist influence. As Governor Warren expressed it:

Any Communist would take the oath and laugh; first, because they are taught to lie about such matters and habitually do lie about them; and, secondly, because if this oath is falsified they could not be punished for it, as it is not an oath required by law.[1]

The counterargument here was: "But though it may not do much good, it will do no harm. Why, then, not sign it and avoid all the other ill consequences?" All that the professor could say in reply to this counterargument was that he was opposed to false fronts in general, and so he usually went on to one of the more important arguments.

This matter of mere inexpediency might be considered of small moment except for one reason. In the long run, the insistence of the regents in demanding what seemed to be a matter of little practical importance one way or the other steadily built up the belief among the faculty that some subtle influence, perhaps sinister, was working beneath the surface. Therefore, as the months passed, what had begun as a struggle against the oath itself became more and more a struggle against the oath as a symbol of something else.

6. University Welfare. By February most members of the faculty had become convinced that the oath was not of pre-eminent importance in itself but that certain of the regents were trying by means of it to force their arbitrary will upon the faculty, destroy any effective faculty autonomy, and thus

---

[1] See San Francisco *Chronicle*, March 1, 1950. What seems to have been the general failure to take the oath seriously is concretely illustrated by what usually happened when a professor, perhaps after months of soul-wrestling, went into the Administration Building to take the oath. There he found a bored secretary doubling as a notary. If he expected his swearing to be solemn and dignified he was disappointed. He was not asked to hold up his right hand. He signed the slip of paper, and the girl threw it on a pile of others. "Aren't you going to stamp it?" he asked. "Oh," she said, "I'll stamp them all later." The professor then left, not even having a receipt.

gain direct control of the University in a way not warranted by the spirit of the Constitutional Act or by tradition. The faculty did not believe that the welfare of the University and of the state would be furthered by the success of such a power drive. Especially after the "Sign-or-get-out!" ultimatum, these thoughts began to loom large and to stiffen resistance. As was only to be expected, the general argument of University welfare focused particularly upon the problem of Academic Tenure.

7. *Academic Tenure.* From the very beginning the faculty had recognized that the imposition of the oath was obviously overthrowing the principle of Academic Tenure. The argument was not complex. As a telling editorial in the *Pacific Spectator* (Spring 1950) declared:

If a professor is required on Monday to sign just this one harmless little oath that wouldn't hurt anybody (or else lose his job), he may equally well be required on Wednesday to do just some other little something (or else lose his job), and then perhaps something very serious (or else lose his job) on Friday. Where, then, is academic freedom?

After February 24 this issue of Academic Tenure intensified and became the immediately dominant one. As the faculty had now come to believe, any admission that the regents could require a particular oath, even if it were not otherwise a serious matter, opened the way for the imposition of any kind of tyrannical requirement upon the Faculty, on penalty of being dismissed without even a hearing.

8. *Academic Freedom.* Since Tenure and Academic Freedom are inseparably bound, the argument against the oath on the basis of Academic Freedom had, from the beginning, run parallel with that on the basis of Tenure. The imposition of the oath, moreover, struck directly at Freedom by setting up a field within which thought was no longer free. Having signed the oath, a professor might still think about Communism, but he necessarily had always to come out with the answer that Communism was bad. "Very well," the

proponents of the oath would say, "we should have only the professors who would come out with that kind of answer." The counterargument, however, would be that there is a difference—theoretical, perhaps, but still important—between a professor who arrives at that conclusion by the exercise of his own freedom of thought and a professor who arrives at that conclusion because he is afraid that if he arrives at any other he will lose his job. There may be, in fact, just the slight difference between an honest man and a hypocrite. And in such a case no one can be absolutely sure that his intellectual honesty may not be swayed by expediency.

In particular, the imposition of the oath injured Academic Freedom from the point of view of the student. Let us consider the student who is experimenting with Communistic ideas, who is even listening to the arguments of Communist propagandists. If his professors have been forced to abjure Communism, these agitators will be quick to seize that weapon. They will say to the student, "Your professors naturally must argue against Communism. They would lose their jobs otherwise. You may be able to trust their opinions on other matters, but obviously not on this." It is difficult to see how the student could fail to accept such a strong argument, and with that acceptance we should have to admit that Academic Freedom had ceased to exist for the student because it had first ceased to exist for the professor.

Having gained some conception of the issues, we may now profitably turn our consideration to the chronological history of the controversy, to what happened month by month during the year.

CHAPTER 4

The History of the Controversy: A Calendar

The history of the controversy breaks into four periods. The first, a prelude, extends from January to May 1949. During these months the regents assumed their position; i.e., they voted the requirement of the oath. During the period from May 1949 to January 4, 1950, the faculty became more and more alive to the threat inherent in the situation, and largely on idealistic grounds took successively stronger positions; the regents tended to be conciliatory. If the faculty had firmly asked in June what it asked in September, or in September what it asked in November, the controversy might have ended at that point. The faculty advance came to a sharp stop on January 4, when the Conference Committee, realizing that they could not obtain the full demands, asked for something less. From January 4 to March 31 the situation of the preceding period was reversed. The regents were anything but conciliatory. They were ready, month by month, to grant less and less. If they had been ready to grant in March what they had refused in January, the controversy might have been ended at that point. The faculty retreated steadily, largely abandoning its idealistic grounds out of sheer economic fear. The period from March 31 to April 21 represents the climax. In these weeks the regents again recognized the necessity of compromise, and thus the faculty and the University escaped the extreme disaster.

PRELUDE: THE REGENTS TAKE A POSITION
(January–May 1949)

January 1949. Comptroller James H. Corley, in his capacity as University representative at the Legislature, recommends to President Robert G. Sproul that an anti-Communist oath be required of the faculty as a preventive to the possible passage of legislation dangerous to the University.

March 25. Regents' meeting. President Sproul presents oath proposal, and it is decided that a reference to the Regents' (1940) anti-Communist policy be added to the constitutional oath of loyalty. A draft of such an oath is presented by the president and unanimously adopted.

May. Faculty Bulletin appears, with the statement that "acceptance letters" for 1949–50 appointments will contain a new oath (text not given) which must be signed before salary checks can be released.

THE FACULTY ADVANCES
(June 7, 1949–January 4, 1950)

June 7. Meeting of Academic Senate (Northern Section). A resolution concerning the oath, of which the text is not yet generally known, is made an order of business for a special meeting to be held a week later.

June 11. The text of the oath is released to the press by President's Office. To the usual pledge of allegiance (Article XX, Section 3, of the California Constitution) is added: "I do not believe in and am not a member of nor do I support any party or organization that believes in, advocates or teaches the overthrow of the United States government by force or violence."

June 14. Special meeting of Academic Senate (Northern Section). Large attendance. Much discussion, and much unity of feeling. General expression of loyalty and of willingness to take the constitutional oath. Objection to special oath, chiefly on grounds of ambiguity, political test, guilt by association, and Academic Freedom. Resolution is passed requesting the president to inform the regents that the members of the' Northern Section, "although unaware of any conduct which warrants doubt about their loyalty and zeal," have no objection to reaffirming their loyalty to the state and nation, but request that the special addition "be deleted or revised in a manner mutually acceptable to the regents and the members of the Academic Senate." Advisory Committee is instructed to consult with the president "with a view to working out such a solution." This resolution is passed in an upsurge of enthusiasm and idealism with only four or five dissenting votes, but it has to be acted on without time for full and proper consideration of all its bearings. In consequence the faculty makes an important parliamentary mistake, which is to vex them later and perhaps fatally to injure their cause; viz., certain members believe the Advisory Committee has been entrusted with power to act, while other members believe that the committee has been given power only to consult and refer the matter back to the Senate.

June 18. Advisory Committee (Northern Section) confers with president and proposes as a first solution the traditional oath plus a statement of University policy on the employment or retention of Communists which faculty members would merely express their acquiescence in. A second solution, to be employed only if "the public relations of the University make an amplification of the [traditional] oath indispensable," might read: "That I am not under oath, nor a party to any agreement, nor as a member of any party or organization am I under any commitment that is in conflict with my obligations under this oath."

June 20. Meeting of the Academic Senate (Southern Section). It adopts the same resolutions as the Northern Section.

June 21. Advisory Committee (Southern Section) confers with the president, later informs him in writing that it concurs with the Advisory Committee (Northern Section).

June 24. Regents' meeting. Resolution is passed reaffirming the 1940 anti-Communist policy and requiring an oath beginning with the constitutional pledge, incorporating the Advisory Committee's suggested words of the second solution, but *inserting* an explicit abjuration of Communist membership; the second part of the oath, which was to stand unchanged throughout the controversy, therefore read: "that I am not a member of the Communist Party, or under any oath, or a party to any agreement, or under any commitment that is in conflict with my obligations under this oath."

June 27. Since the regular session of the University has now ended, and since many professors are absent, teaching at other summer sessions, or following their research in the field, no regular meeting of the Senate can be held. This fact has two serious results. (1) It inspires the suspicion that the whole matter may thus have been timed in order to isolate the faculty members individually and thus put them at a disadvantage. (2) In the absence of Senate meetings, smaller groups of the faculty naturally begin to meet for the study of possibilities and mutual support and these groups probably take less conciliatory positions than they might have taken if a Senate meeting had been possible. On June 27 the first "non-signers" meeting is held at the Faculty Club in Berkeley. This group takes the position that new oath is not essentially better than old one, that Advisory Committee was not given power to act, and that individual Senate members are therefore not bound by the committee's action. The mutter of "Sold down the river!" (a favorite one throughout the rest of the year) is first heard. The non-signers concentrate for immediate action upon securing separation of the oath from the letters of acceptance for the new year and postponement of the deadline until fall.

June 28. The chairman of the Advisory Committee discusses the ideas of the non-signers with President Sproul.

June 30. Unofficial statement by "University officials" in the press that salary checks will not be held up.

July 6. Non-Senate academic employees meet, organize, and support the Senate position opposing the oath. (This group continued to meet throughout the year and to maintain a firm stand. As stated in Chapter I, however, its activities cannot be detailed in the present work.)

July 8. First meeting of "non-signers" held in Los Angeles. (During the summer this group kept in touch with the similar group in Berkeley, and in general parallel actions were taken.) Everywhere this is a time of considerable disunion in the faculty. There are recriminations by the non-signers against the signers and the Advisory Committee, and vice versa.

Mid-July. The president sends letters to the faculty individually, presenting the regents' resolution of June 24, appending the oath to be signed, and expressing his hope that it would be signed and returned by October 1. (The conciliatory tone of the letter caused October 1 to be known later as "the soft deadline.") A considerable number sign the revised oath. Some of these sympathize with the regents' action. Others have no great objection and sign merely to get the matter off their minds and be able to continue regular work. Others sign because the oath has come to them while they are absent from Berkeley and, lacking other information, they assume that the Senate has concurred in this form of the oath. Still others sign because they feel that, by the action of the Senate on June 24, the Advisory Committee had been empowered to act.

Late July. It becomes obvious that contracts for 1949–50 are being sent out only to signers. The faculty considers this a breach of faith (see under June 30), and there is great indignation. This is a major strategic mistake on the regent-administration side (the two were at this time generally allied). This "high-pressuring" of the faculty at a time when there was no possibility of a Senate meeting effects its reunification. As a result of many protests, monthly checks are shortly sent to non-signers also.

August. Since there is no possibility of a Senate meeting and since there are no immediate matters that can be solved, this is a quiet month.

September 19. Senate meeting (Northern Section), approximately 650 voting members present. The president states that the regents' resolution of June 24 is "aimed at the Communist Party alone" and that no non-Communist faculty member "who regards the regents' policy as unwise will 'be deemed to have severed his connection with the University.'" He promises, for non-signers, "the traditional consultation with the Committee on Privilege and Tenure." He announces that to date slightly more than half of the academic personnel on the northern campuses of the University have signed the oath. (He makes, however, no breakdown of these statistics as between Senate members and non-Senate academic employees. Most members of the Senate therefore hold to the belief that fewer than half of their members have signed.) University Regulation No. 5 is read (see Appendix A). Two resolutions are passed (see Appendix A). The first pledges wholehearted concurrence with Regulation No. 5, interpreted to prohibit "the employment of persons whose commitments or obligations to any organization, Communist or other, prejudice impartial scholarship and the free pursuit of truth." (The words inside the commas were the critical ones. It was hoped, although this hope was not expressed in so many words, that the inclusion of the word "Communist" would satisfy the regents and that the inclusion of the words "or other" would satisfy those who objected on the grounds of "political test" or "guilt by association." This may be described as a forlorn semantic hope.) In a second resolution, the Senate requested for its members the privilege of subscribing voluntarily to the constitutional oath, and thus, by implication, to no other.

September 22. Meeting of the Academic Senate (Southern Section). Resolutions substantially the same as those adopted in Berkeley are presented. Discussion reveals that these resolutions were originally framed by the southern committee and that the Southern Section could therefore not be considered as performing a mere rubber-stamp action. After some heated discussion the resolutions are passed. (By the actions of September 19 and 22 the Senate shifted from its "delete or revise" position of June to its later consistently held position—"delete." Although this was widely interpreted by the regents and others as a power drive or "repudiation" or mere uncertainty of mind, it may also be interpreted as showing that the faculty members had become much more aware of the implications of the oath because of many discussions during "The Hundred Days" which intervened between Senate meetings.)

September 23. Regents' meeting. The faculty resolutions are presented. A committee is appointed to confer with the Advisory Committees.

September 29. This conference is held in San Francisco. The faculty representatives orally state the Senate's views and also present fifteen key documents in order to place the case in the record. After more than four hours of discussion the faculty representatives withdraw, not without hope that the Regents' Committee has not unsympathetically entertained the faculty point of view. (The faculty representatives were to be astonished at the next day's meeting.)

September 30. Regents' meeting. The Special Committee of the Regents presents, as a result of deliberation which followed the withdrawal of the faculty representatives on September 29, an entirely negative and completely unyielding set of recommendations. The faculty representatives then argue their case again. The Board makes some qualifications; viz., (1) that the letters of contract be released, (2) that an informal affirmation be acceptable instead of the formal oath. The regents express themselves ready for further negotiation, and a semblance of unity is preserved by the statement that there is "complete agreement upon the objectives of the University policy excluding members of the Communist Party." This last is, however, another semantic trap. The faculty representatives emphasized *objectives;* the regents, *policy*. The difference of emphasis involved the oath and the acceptance of guilt by association rather than personal guilt. Some of the regents may not have seen the semantic distinction; others may have pretended not to see it, either tacitly accepting the faculty position or biding their time for charges of "equivocation" and "second repudiation." By the end of the meeting tempers are strained. The Board having granted that a faculty member may sign an "equivalent" to the oath, a reporter asks just what is meant. The chairman snaps, "Look up *equivalent* in the dictionary!" As others rise with questions, he bangs his gavel. "Meeting adjourned!" (In spite of innumerable recourses to lexicographers' masterpieces, however, the question of what the regents meant by "equivalent" remained uncertain, and many professors who signed what they themselves considered to be an equivalent found themselves left dangling). . . . Since this is the last day before "the soft deadline," many faculty members, driven by economic insecurity, sign their oaths.

October 7, 25, and November 14. Meetings of the Academic Senate (Southern Section). *October 10, and November 7.* Meetings of the Academic Senate (Northern Section). These long meetings, chiefly devoted to discussion, need not be individually presented in detail. The Advisory Committees report, and on their motion the Senate votes "complete agreement upon the objectives of the University [anti-Communist] policy." On another motion of the Advisory Committees a Conference Committee is appointed to continue the negotiations with the regents. Its instructions are essentially: (1) "Delete," (2) Do not commit the Senate to approval of what the special oath stands for; i.e., political test and guilt by association. The Adams Resolution (see Appendix A for pertinent part) is presented by Professor G. P. Adams and passed.

November 30. The Berkeley non-signers effect a permanent but informal organization. (They continue to meet from time to time until after April 21. This courageous and highly idealistic, though loquacious, group exercised a not inconsiderable influence on general faculty opinion and helped to direct the conscientious objections of its own members along co-operative and strategic lines.)

December 13. Chairmen of Conference Committee meet with Regent Neylan, chairman of the Regents' Committee, to present the Senate's position, but find themselves mostly listening to an expression of the regent's position.

December 16. Regents' meeting. Fox dismissed (see Chapter 5).

January 4, 1950. Conference Committee meets with Regents' Committee and makes proposal centering around acceptance of existing procedures whereby men are judged by their peers on the basis of individual competence and character. The regents' objections focus upon the Communist issue; their attack is directed at what they call the two "repudiations" by the Senate of its committees, and at "the dissident minority," as they term the non-signers. With their proposal seeming certain to be rejected, the Conference Committees try to save something by offering some slight compromises.

THE FACULTY RETREATS
(January 4, 1950–March 31, 1950)

January 12. Regents' Committee meets and apparently[1] divides evenly on whether to accept the Conference Committee's proposals.

[1]Official regents' records are not all available to the authors of this book. See Chapter 12.

January 13. Regents' meeting. Regents' Committee is discharged. Conference Committee is instructed to address future communications to president. This Regents' meeting shows the Senate advance on an idealistic basis definitely ended, and the Senate retreat on a materialistic (economic) basis definitely begun.

February. Conference Committee, recognizing inevitability of more explicit recognition of the anti-Communist policy, offers a compromise through the president: that the annual contracts contain a statement of the non-Communist policy and that the faculty member accept his position subject to this condition of employment, without thereby expressing his personal approval of that policy.

February 24. Regents' meeting. A statement presented over signatures of forty-two deans and chairmen of departments and Senate committees, indicating the ensuing damage to the University if loyal men are dismissed only for failure to sign the oath is read and disregarded. It is dismissed by one regent as the work of "campus politicians." The Board votes by twelve to six[2] that those not signing by April 30 would automatically be deemed to have severed their connection with the University as of June 30. This comes to be known immediately as "The Sign-or-Get-Out Ultimatum."

February 25. Much perturbation on all campuses of the University. Faculty members begin to realize that the fight has shifted out of ideology and become a struggle for some degree of Academic Freedom. After three lengthy meetings with deans and department chairmen, the Conference Committee decides to carry on as an operating agency, until the next Senate meeting, to conduct a publicity campaign and prepare for legal defense.

February 27. Non-signers' meeting with attendance of 150 at Berkeley. General feeling that the break between regents

[2]Yes: Ahlport, Dickson, Ehrman, Giannini, Hale, Jordan, McFadden, Merchant, Neylan, Pauley, Sprague, Teague.
No: Fenston, Griffiths, Hansen, Heller, Sproul, Warren.

and faculty is open and irretrievable. Nearly all present express their determination to stand together and accept dismissal rather than sign the oath.

February 28. Faculty defense fund inaugurated.

March 6. Mass meeting of students in Berkeley to hear the issue discussed. Regent Neylan unable to attend because of "badly neglected cold" but sends a message, which seems to be an olive branch. He asks, "As a constructive step toward the solution of this situation, why does the Academic Senate not adopt a resolution in plain English unequivocally endorsing the policy excluding Communists?"

March 7. Meeting of the Academic Senate (Northern Section). (Historians in the Senate recall that this day was one hundred years, to the day, after the famous compromising session of the United States Senate on March 7, 1850.) After hearing a report of the Conference Committee's defeat and its request to be relieved, the Senate votes, defiantly and unanimously, a resolution rejecting "the special oath, and the arbitrary dismissal of loyal members of the faculty for refusal to sign this oath." It decides to vote by secret mail ballot upon two propositions. Proposition #1, presented by the Conference Committee, provides that faculty members, in addition to taking the constitutional oath, shall henceforth indicate acceptance of the regents' anti-Communist policy as explicitly set forth in future contracts. Proposition #2, moved from the floor, proposes the adoption by the faculty itself of the policy that "proved members of the Communist Party, by reason of such commitments to that party, are not acceptable as members of the faculty." (See Appendix A for texts.) In a large informal meeting of faculty, held immediately after Senate meeting, plans for the fight are announced, and the appointment of an operating Committee of Seven is authorized.

March 8. Meeting of Academic Senate (Southern Section). Similar actions are taken. . . . The Committees of Seven (North and South) take over. . . . Regent Neylan in a press release hails with delight the March 7 actions: "With the regents and the faculty united . . . we shall solve all our problems."

March 3–21. Telegrams, letters, and contributions of money pour in from university faculties and from private individuals all over the country, and from abroad, in support of the faculty stand. Many of these letters are released to the press. The controversy is front-page news and editorial material throughout the state. . . . More conservative and cautious faculty members urge heavy vote for Proposition ⚹2, feeling that this acceptance of Regent Neylan's olive branch provides only way to prevent wholesale dismissals and save University.

March 22. Results of vote on the two propositions are announced: Proposition ⚹1. Northern Section: Yes, 841; No, 93; Abstaining, 15. Southern Section: Yes, 313; No, 43; Abstaining, 18. Proposition ⚹2. Northern Section: Yes, 724; No, 203; Abstaining, 22. Southern Section: Yes, 301; No, 65; Abstaining, 8. The results are viewed by many of the faculty as a relinquishment, albeit under duress, of fundamental civil and academic liberties. The vote is taken to mean the end of controversy, and this seems to be borne out by statements of the regents. Regent Neylan greets the result by calling it a clear meeting of the issue of "civilization versus barbarism," by congratulating the faculty for being the first in the United States to take this stand, and by agreeing that the solution of the controversy is at hand.

March 31. Regents' meeting. In what observers have described as "four and a half hours of bitter, table-pounding debate," Regent Neylan, despite his earlier statement, again leads attack against faculty position. Faculty representatives read compromise proposal. Regents split ten to ten on a motion to withdraw the ultimatum.[3] This tie vote permits the

[3]Yes (i.e., pro-Faculty): Ehrman, Fenston, Griffiths, Haggerty, Hansen, Heller, Simpson, Sproul, Steinhart, Warren.
No: Ahlport, Collins, Dickson, Giannini, Jordan, Knight, McFadden, Merchant, Neylan, Sprague.

ultimatum to stand. This meeting is known in faculty circles as the Santa Barbara Meeting, the Meeting of March 31, or the Great Double-Cross.

THE CLIMAX (March 31, 1950–April 21, 1950)

April 1. The faculty, although worn down by long battle, rapidly splitting into splinter groups under the pressures of defeat, and well-nigh hopeless for themselves and for the University, rallies as best it can behind the Committee of Seven. Non-signers generally stand firm, although some admit that they are "April 30 men." Some signers write to the president requesting the return of oaths, so that they may stand with the non-signers. Others declare that they will resign if anyone is dismissed merely for failure to sign the oath. The dominant issues are now Academic Freedom and Tenure. It is felt that a certain group of regents is ready to wreck a strong University in order to gain absolute control over what would be left. A "Sign, stay, and fight" movement also develops, gaining strength from the feeling that it is better to sign the oath and then remain to fight for the restoration of the University's freedom. Although preparations for legal defense continue, and although a moderate publicity campaign is maintained, the strategy of the Committee of Seven shifts toward influencing certain regents who are thought to be a little shaky.

April 4. Work begins on the present book.

April 7. Violent anti-faculty statement is released by Regents Dickson, Giannini, and Neylan: "Preparations are being made once more to intimidate the regents."

April 15. Announcement by Regent Hale (president of the Alumni Association) that the California Alumni Association is actively at work on the problem through a committee.

April 18. Press release that 245 faculty members and other employees of Stanford University have signed a letter supporting the University of California faculty and accompanied it with substantial contributions to the defense fund.

April 20. University of Chicago faculty votes a 2-per-cent voluntary contribution of its salary to support the University of California faculty. Action involving financial support is also initiated by faculty committees at Columbia, Cornell, Duke, Harvard, Illinois, Michigan, New York University, Northwestern, Ohio State, Pennsylvania, Princeton, Roosevelt College, Sarah Lawrence College, Vanderbilt, Wisconsin, Yale, and perhaps other universities and colleges.

April 21. Regents' meeting. Regents vote (twenty-one to one) to rescind the requirement of the oath. Its essentials are, however, transferred to the body of the annual contract. Failure to sign the material as there included will not be cause for summary dismissal, as a hearing before the Faculty Committee on Privilege and Tenure is authorized. (See Appendix A for text.) Regent Giannini, having cast the only negative vote, resigns. Most faculty members accept the vote as a last-minute reprieve and a breathing spell. The position of the faculty remains, however, much worse than it was a year previous. The conviction is general that this is merely the end of the first campaign, not the end of a war.

This bare skeleton is presented merely that the reader may have some idea of the chronology and the external events. In the whole controversy, the issue of Communism was constantly involved, particularly in the minds of the anti-faculty regents. This delicate matter calls for more detailed presentation in the next chapter.

CHAPTER 5

The T.A. and the Piano Player

A T.A., in the language of the University of California campuses, is a teaching assistant—a part-time graduate student and part-time instructional helper, a sort of academic non-commissioned officer, holding his place between the privates first-class, who are the graduate students, and the second lieutenants, who are the instructors.

A piano player, in anyone's language, is a piano player.

The one great irony that underlies all the long-drawn and bitter oath controversy is that the only actual charges of Communism were leveled at one teaching assistant and one piano player. Not a single professor was so charged, even in the heat of the discussion; not one Senate member, North or South.

Let us review the situation. . . . In 1940, after dismissing one teaching assistant as being a Communist, the regents declared that "membership in the Communist Party is incompatible with membership in the faculty of a state university." At that time Stalin was allied with Hitler, and the situation was tense. After that, for nine years, the regents made no charges of Communism.

In 1949 they applied the anti-Communist policy to all employees, not merely to the faculty, and required that everyone sign the oath. On September 30, 1949, responding to a protest from the Senate, the regents announced that they would not withdraw the oath until the Senate could suggest a "further or better implementation of the policy." But the regents did not explain why the anti-Communist policy needed implementation. They had not, for nine years, pointed to a single Communist.

On this same day, September 30, however, came the first suggestion during the oath controversy that there might be a real and not just some imaginary Communists somewhere on the University pay roll. In the regents' meeting, Regent Neylan inquired regarding "a teaching assistant named Fox, who, I read in the papers, refused to testify in Washington as to whether he was a Communist." (San Francisco *Chronicle*, October 1, 1949.) During all the later stages of the oath controversy the name Fox has stood as a kind of symbol. We have talked of "the Fox case." We have tended to forget that Irving David Fox, the T.A., is just as real a person as any professor. It is not good thus to lose the human touch.

THE T.A.

Mr. Fox is a man of thirty, looking slightly younger. He is a little above medium height, with auburn hair, brown eyes, and the fine, clear complexion that occasionally goes with such coloring. He is definitely a handsome fellow, with quiet voice and good manners. He is married, has one child, and is now looking, under considerable handicap, for a job.

He was employed at the University Radiation Laboratory (the Cyclotron, to the public) from 1942 to 1945. He then spent a year in the Navy. In 1946 he returned briefly to the same laboratory, and later in the same year began his service as a teaching assistant in the Physics Department at Berkeley.

In September 1949 he was one of several witnesses who appeared before the House Un-American Activities Committee during its investigation of alleged Communist infiltration at the Radiation Laboratory; his refusal to answer certain questions was reported in the papers, and he thus came to the attention of Regent Neylan.

In November the regents decided to notify Mr. Fox that at their next meeting they would "give consideration to your status in the University of California in view of the testimony that you gave, or declined to give, before the House Un-American Activities Committee on September 27, 1949." (Transcript of regents' meeting, December 16, 1949.)

On December 16, at an open regents' meeting, Fox appeared before the Board. The regents inquired why he had refused to answer certain questions during the congressional hearing—"on the grounds that it might tend to incriminate me." (See Hearing before House Comm. on Un-Amer. Activities of Scientist X, 81st Cong., 1st Sess.) Among questions which he had refused to answer were the following: "Have you ever been a member of the Communist Party of the United States?" "Were you a member of the Communist cell at the Radiation Laboratory?" "Was your father a member of the Communist Party?"

Fox explained that he had refused to answer these questions at the congressional hearing on advice of counsel. "I would not have been against testifying on most of the questions," he stated, "but a sort of unpleasant situation exists today with regard to the Communist Party and being associated with the Communist Party, and Mr. Durr [Fox's lawyer] possibly was overcautious on this. . . . He felt it would be better if I did answer the questions, but there was always the possibility of persecution on this basis, and he felt that all things considered—— [Here Regent Neylan interrupted, and this sentence was never finished]." (See transcript of the regents' meeting, December 16, 1949.)

Fox told the regents that in the late thirties he was a member of what might be labeled Communist-front organizations, that in 1942 he had attended Communist Party meetings, that "as far as my membership or lack of membership, I was to all intents and purposes—I was a participant. Officially I believe I was not a member, but that was only a fine distinction of course. I did actually participate in their organization. However, I never signed a membership card." Concluding, he stated that in 1942 "I began to feel that this was not the organization for me." The year of his final break with the Communists was "possibly 1942 and possibly 1943" because "I decided I did not agree with them."

Fox's statements to the regents and his replies to Regent Neylan's questions fill fifteen typed pages single-spaced. He can thus scarcely be accused of having been unwilling to talk. He would not answer Regent Neylan's questions as to the associations and beliefs of other persons, but every other question he seems to have discussed freely and frankly.

At the end he was told: "It would be a good idea to wait." After a brief executive session he was notified of the regents' decision that he "be dismissed from the service of the University on a finding that he does not meet the minimum requirements for membership on the faculty." (*Fac. Bull.*, v. 19, #7, Jan. 1950) He was handed a lump-sum payment ($840) covering his teaching assistant's salary until the end of his one-year appointment; i.e., until June 30, 1950.

The Fox case naturally aroused great interest, even excitement, throughout the University, and there was much adverse comment upon the vagueness of the unexplained "minimum requirements." Perhaps for this reason the regents, or some of them, felt that their position was weak. In any case, they considered Fox again in January and issued a further statement. (See *Fac. Bull.*, v. 19, #8, Feb. 1950; also *Amer. Civ. Lib. Un. News*, v. 15, #4, Apr. 1950.)

They now noted that Fox was not a member of the faculty but only a "teaching" employee, and presumably, therefore, not entitled to the full explanation of his case that is the right of a member of the faculty. Nevertheless, they made some explanation, stressing three points; viz., Fox's refusal to answer the questions of the congressional committee, his former associations with the Communist movement, and his activity with two persons who, the regents seem to believe, were Communists trying to control the personnel of the Radiation Laboratory. The statement reiterated that Fox was dismissed from the University "on the ground he did not meet minimum requirements for membership in its teaching departments."

Apparently, then, the "minimum requirements" are bound up in some way with the three matters listed above.

These requirements were not apparently related to efficient service, for there is no suggestion in the regents' statement that the professors and deans who appointed Fox in 1946, 1947, 1948, and 1949 erred in judging his teaching ability. Further, there is no suggestion that he violated the University requirement that its teachers should not be Communists. His admission that in years prior to his appointment as a teaching assistant he had been a member of a Communist movement "to all intents and purposes" is twice noted, but the regents nowhere impugn his statement that he had cut off all such associations, ideological and other, at least three years prior to 1946, when he first became a teaching assistant. He had, moreover, signed the special oath, and the regents do not suggest or imply that he had not signed it in good faith.

Perhaps the regents are in a difficult position. Perhaps they know more about Fox than they feel it politic, in the best interests of the University, to announce. Nevertheless, this sudden conjuring up of these "minimum requirements," really undefined, is suspiciously like passing a law to suit the special case before the bar.

Are there any bounds on the power of the regents thus to fix requirements—in vague language—suddenly, without warning? If the regents have this power to create new requirements while judging individual cases, is there any guarantee of protection to the faculty? These particular questions have not been answered by the rescinding of the oath requirement, nor by the other actions of the regents on April 21, 1950.

Fair trial in a university, as in a democracy, demands that an offense charged against a man be clearly stated, so that he may prepare his defense and answer the evidence used against him. As Chief Justice Hughes declared in 1938: "The right to a hearing embraces not only the right to present evidence but also a reasonable opportunity to know the claims of the opposing party and to meet them." (Morgan v. United States, 304 U.S. 1, 1938). The offense charged against Fox was not clearly stated, and even now we are unsure as to just what was the regulation of the regents that he may have violated.

Unless his case is *sui generis,* bitter struggles can be forecast within the University of California.

THE PIANO PLAYER

"I've sold my piano," ran a bitter saying in faculty circles during the spring of 1950, "it was too dangerous to have around." This saying couples the idea of "guilt by association" and the case of the piano player.

Like Irving David Fox, Mrs. Miriam Brooks Sherman is not merely a symbol but must also be considered a human being. We have not been able to talk with her, but we have an eight-page, single-spaced, typewritten statement from her.[1] Her first paragraph reads:

I have been employed as a Pianist for the Department of Physical Education for Women, UCLA, since July 1, 1946. The position is non-academic, and was not clearly defined until Dec., 1949, in the Personnel Manual, which states: Duties are to "play piano for dance and exercise classes and for entertainments."

Mrs. Sherman, with some pride, points out that her duties were really more extensive than this, but she makes no claim to having instructed classes.

On March 1, 1950, a few days after the regents' meeting in which the "Sign-or-get-out!" ultimatum was adopted over the dissenting votes of Governor Warren, President Sproul, and four other regents, newspapers carried a press statement by State Senator Jack B. Tenney, former chairman of the Senate Fact-Finding Committee on Un-American Activities. Tenney took this opportunity to announce that he had uncovered a Communist Party member on the University pay roll and was preparing a letter to President Sproul, naming the person and

[1]All quotations attributed to Mrs. Sherman in this chapter are from this statement.

giving proofs. This newspaper story, however, had no immediate follow-up.

On March 13, according to her own story, Mrs. Sherman was summoned before Dean D. F. Jackey of the College of Applied Arts. He asked her various questions as to possible Communist connections, and she refused to answer, standing on her "personal and constitutional rights." To another question as to whether Mrs. Eleanor Pasternak, an assistant supervisor in the Department of Physical Education for Women, was her sister, Mrs. Sherman replied, "Most certainly, yes."

In the week before the meeting at which the regents were being asked to rescind their ultimatum, the newspapers identified Senator Tenney's "Communist" as Mrs. Sherman.

On the three days preceding the regents' meeting various newspapers played up the case, with the obvious intent, it is to be feared, of bringing pressure to bear upon the regents not to rescind the oath—and with, it is also to be feared, that result. At least, on March 31, several of the regents who were supporting the maintenance of the ultimatum referred to Mrs. Sherman as demonstrating the need for the oath.

On April 20 the case ended in what must be considered from the point of view of the oath controversy—though not perhaps for Mrs. Sherman—a sudden anticlimax. Mrs. Sherman's sister held an academic position in the same department, and a University regulation forbids such "nepotism." On this day, therefore, at eleven forty-five, Mrs. Sherman was called from the middle of a "Rhythms" class and was informed that since her employment was in violation of that regulation she was dismissed, effective immediately, with pay for the remainder of the contract year. She was directed to leave the campus immediately, without completing the work scheduled for her for the remainder of the day.

Unlike the Fox case, the Sherman case creates no precedent and probably leaves behind it no problem. Whether knowingly or not, Mrs. Sherman was violating an established University regulation and was therefore subject to dismissal. There is, of course, something comically pusillanimous in this sudden bundling of her off the campus in the middle of a class, while all the girls on the gymnasium floor, we are left to imagine, stood poised on one toe, waiting for the concluding chords that never came.

Mrs. Sherman's position in the University was even more suburban than that of Mr. Fox. His position was academic and might be called quasi-faculty. But Mrs. Sherman was not even on the edge of the faculty; she was hardly within shouting distance. The position of the faculty as to the existence of Communists in their ranks therefore remains still wholly unimpeached.

As some disillusioned wit among us has remarked: "The special oath seems to be an ineffective means of getting rid of Communists—who aren't there to begin with!"

CHAPTER 6

Power Drive Against the University

The constitutional position of the University of California is excellent. Its Board of Regents is established in the California Constitution as an independent unit of state government, responsible neither to the governor nor to the Legislature. The Legislature retains the privilege of granting or withholding funds, and thus has potentially something of a whip hand. Nevertheless, the position of the regents is extremely strong, and the University is thus spared direct interference from the Legislature.

A great and primary function of the Board of Regents as originally conceived was to stand as a buffer between the faculty, who should be concerned with the eternal truths, and the various vociferous or subtle pressure groups, each assuming to speak with the voice of the people. In the nineteenth century these pressure groups often raised their voices and accused the University of being "godless" and "impractical." In later years the charges brought against University professors have often involved economic thought, and in the letter written by Regent Rowell in 1921 (see Chapter 2) we have an excellent example of a regent in his highest function, that of defending Academic Freedom against such clamorous attack. Too often, moreover, no really conscientious motives can be assigned to these groups clamoring against the University; they must be considered merely to be working for their own private purposes in "power drives" designed to gain control of the University for some immediate end.

No date this side of 1868 need be assigned as "first" in this history. We can start almost anywhere. The depth of the depression is as good a time as any, and the campaign of the large agricultural interests furnishes as good an example as any.

When migrant cotton pickers struck in 1933, a half dozen students marched in the picket lines, and a member of the University faculty joined with colleagues on the governor's Fact-Finding Commission in recommending an increase of wages to the pickers. Thereupon a county supervisor complained that "taxpayers furnish money to educate young radicals"; a newspaper objected to the alleged "Communistic" character of "preachments in the lecture halls of our universities," and the editor of the *Pacific Rural Press* said that "many college professors believe they represent pure science and no person or class . . . But these are new days, with imperative new needs." The threat of a cut in the University budget was raised.

During the thirties the efforts of agricultural workers to organize themselves stirred employing interests in California deeply and moved them to resistance. In the name of combating Communism the Associated Farmers was established among agricultural employers in 1934 and financed primarily by industrial, financial, railroad, utility, and processing interests. Family-size farmers were conspicuous by their scarcity in the councils of the organization. In 1936 the Associated Farmers began to promote the view that the patriotism of California's educational institutions was questionable and to demand that teachers and college professors be required to take oaths.

However patriotic the emotions and intentions of those who sponsored and led the Associated Farmers, some of their activities were of a character that attracted the attention of the Civil Liberties Committee of the United States Senate. Concluding an extended examination, the senators found that "the record of the organization and activities of the Associated

Farmers from 1935 to 1940 presents a challenge to democratic government in California and the Nation," and is one of "conspiracy," "executed ruthlessly," "designed to prevent the exercise of their civil liberties by oppressed wage laborers in agriculture."

It would be going too far, of course, to assert that the Associated Farmers, as an organization, or even that any of its individual members dictated or furnished persistent support behind the demand for a special oath at the University of California. Yet some connection was not wholly absent.

Among the pro-oath regents, for instance, C. C. Teague—a large citrus grower—had been prominent as a raiser of funds and builder of support for the Associated Farmers. According to evidence before the Senate committee, another of these pro-oath regents, J. F. Neylan, by his recommendation as attorney, secured a grant of twenty-five hundred dollars from Safeway chain groceries to the Associated Farmers for the purpose of conducting an "educational expansion campaign." Apparently this was the program that the Senate committee said was intended "to spread the ideology of the Associated Farmers throughout the West Coast, through the Intermountain and Midwest territory, to Texas and Florida in the South, and eventually as far East as the Atlantic Seaboard States." The committee expressed its concern over the "scope and seriousness" of this "all-pervasive program of national expansion."

During the 1940s instances began to multiply of drives against education in general and the University of California in particular. The usual ingredients seemed to be strong affirmations of patriotism, with undertones of political and economic interest. In this year Assemblyman Jack Tenney announced that the Legislature would be requested to grant authority to investigate alleged Communistic influences in the University, and for other purposes. In January 1941, Assemblymen Tenney, Phillips (an organizer of the Associated Farmers), and Bashore asked the Legislature for a joint committee to investigate, among other matters, the activities of persons and groups suspected of being foreign-dominated at schools and colleges, including the University of California. Another resolution was introduced for a joint committee to determine "whether members of Communist or Nazi groups are employed as teachers or administrators, and to determine what extent, if any, advocates of political and social philosophies opposed to the democratic form of government are propagandizing minors under the protection of appointive positions over which the voting public has no control." The two resolutions were consolidated, and a Committee on Un-American Activities was established with instructions to include state educational institutions in its investigations.

In its first report, in 1942, this committee said it was convinced that "Communism is not being taught in the universities, or in any of our public schools throughout California." The committee believed, however, that "a considerable number of instructors and faculty members" were either members of the Communist Party or else "fellow travelers." No proofs were presented. The report concluded: "The situation, in the opinion of your committee, is one that can be best handled by the Legislature rather than directly by the University itself."

At last, in the early months of 1949, Tenney, now a member of the Senate, touched off the oath controversy by introducing a bill which would have caused a constitutional amendment to be presented to the people. This amendment would have struck at the autonomy of the University under the regents and would have introduced legislative control of loyalty.

At this point the University's legislative agent decided that the University could best combat the threat by running for cover. The requirement of a special oath was proposed to the regents, and the prelude to the Year of the Oath began.

How unnecessary it all was is shown by the fate of Tenney's bills, in the shifts of politics. Some of them received approval from a legislative committee or even from one house of the Legislature. That was all!

This complete collapse of the Tenney campaign, moreover, came before the oath controversy had become very heated. At the meeting of the Northern Section of the Academic Senate on June 14, President Sproul announced his belief that none of this anti-University legislation had any chance of passing the Legislature. Nevertheless, the regents would not rescind the requirement of the oath, and things went from bad to worse.

We might then well inquire why—the original cause being removed—certain of the regents continued, with almost fanatical vehemence, to insist on the oath.

1. Perhaps some regents believed sincerely—however mistakenly and naïvely—that the University had some Communists, and that the oath supplied a good means of getting rid of them.

2. The regents, having required the oath, naturally did not enjoy backing down before faculty pressure.

Of these two reasons, the first may be considered noble, even if not particularly understandable, and the second understandable, even if not particularly noble. But other possible reasons for the continuation of the oath controversy and for its intensification can scarcely be given even so much justification.

3. On the part of some regents, the controversy apparently developed into a power drive to take over direct control of the University. The actions of these regents would indicate that they wished to establish their right to rule the faculty absolutely, under pain of dismissal, and that they conceived of themselves as employers and of the faculty as employees.

4. Moreover—one might even say necessarily—the drive of these regents against the faculty developed into a drive against the president of the University. Documentation on this point cannot be given. Naturally, it is not a matter that any regent would be likely to shout from the housetops or tell in a press release. Nevertheless, especially after President Sproul lined up on the faculty side at the meeting of February 24, he

stood in the road of this drive on the part of the anti-faculty regents.

5. Almost certainly state politics entered the picture. During the Year of the Oath the campaigns of 1950 were shaping up. Governor Earl Warren, a candidate for re-election, espoused the faculty cause, and his political opponents within his own party went in on the other side. At the Santa Barbara meeting the lieutenant governor and the Speaker of the Assembly, ex officio members of the Board, appeared unexpectedly (see Chapter 12) and voted in opposition to the governor.

6. The sectionalism of the state also played an important part. Although much of the University's strength resides in its state-wide character, there has always been a certain desire on the part of some residents of southern California to have the University of California at Los Angeles a completely independent institution. Since one of the chief obstacles to this separation has been the personality of President Sproul, any attack upon him is almost necessarily to be construed as gaining some support from these separatists. Of the thirteen appointive regents voting in the ten-to-ten vote of March 31, six northern regents voted pro-faculty, and two voted anti-faculty. One southern regent voted pro-faculty, and four voted anti-faculty.

In view of all these extraneous issues that were drawn into the oath controversy, the members of the faculty can scarcely be blamed in thinking that the University was being made a mere pawn and that self-seeking careerists were driving ahead ruthlessly against Academic Freedom.

Others, as well, held the same opinion, and we may quote the words of the editor of the (AFL) East Bay *Labor Journal* (April 7, 1950):

Labor's been through this many times. Hang tough is the motto labor's adopted as a result. Compromise when hell freezes over when you're dealing with Neylan's kind.

What's Neylan up to? Maybe this: He and his gang of re-
actionaries may be trying to mess up things in the State
institutions during the primary campaign in an effort to
weaken Governor Warren so he won't show up too marvel-
,ously well in the primary vote. Then Warren would figure he
had to play ball completely with the most reactionary wing of
his Republican Party. . . .

Note that "Goody" Knight, the lieutenant governor who was
used by the ultra-reactionaries to try to bluff Warren some
months ago, was one of the Regents who voted with Neylan.
And [of] course Giannini of the Bank of America. . . .

But whatever the political implications of Neylan's maneu-
vers may be, tough old organized labor gives you academic
boys and girls of the faculty this advice in two brief words:
Hang tough!

The going was hard for the "academic boys and girls," and
the atmosphere of those months was not friendly to cold logic
or clear processes of the intellect. On June 14, 1949, the day
when the Academic Senate met first in Berkeley to consider
the oath, these were among the headlines in the San Francisco
Chronicle: "ATOM INQUIRY," " 'ARE YOU A COMMUNIST?' "
"RUSS ANSWER U.S. BRITISH BALKAN NOTES," "HISS PER-
JURY TRIAL," "CONDON TO BE CALLED IN COPLON TRIAL,"
"U.N. OFFICIAL SOTIROV DENIES HE'S RUSS AGENT," "BUSI-
NESS VIEW OF RED CHINA," "U.C. LOYALTY OATH NEW
PLEDGE SCHEDULED FOR HEATED DEBATE IN ACADEMIC
SENATE TODAY," "THREE LOYALTY OATHS IN U.C. CONTRO-
VERSY," " 'DANGEROUS IDEAS' AND WELLESLEY," "U. OF ILLI-
NOIS SAYS ITS LOYALTY OATH IS 10 YEARS OLD," "MARYLAND
PROFESSORS MUST SIGN BY JULY 1," "PHI BETA KAPPA OP-
POSED TO OATH," "TWO PUBLIC ISSUES, PRO AND CON Should
Schools Let Communists Be Teachers? Should the FBI Secret
Files Be Used in Court?", "COMMUNISTS COMPLAIN AT N.Y.
TRIAL," "SUPREME COURT TO RULE ON L.A. ANTI-COMMU-
NIST LAW," "THE HAWAII CIO LONGSHORE STRIKE," "CANA-
DIAN CREW PICKETS SHIP HERE," "COAL MINING ENDS LEWIS
TALKS WITH OWNERS," "RUSSIA AND CHINESE COMMUNISTS."

In the midst of such whirlwinds, blowing from all the ends of the earth, the faculty of the University of California tried to raise a voice in the cause of the freedom of the human mind. Small wonder that that voice was not heard clearly! Our own regents, who under the spirit of our old charter should have fought our fight, had pinned the label of disloyalty upon us by requiring of us an oath. Some of them, individually, went farther and implied that there were many Communists in our ranks and that we were being swayed by some vague but sinister "dissident minority." What chance then was there for deliberation, for even tempers, for clear thinking, and for sensible judgments on eternal values, in a period when this whirlwind of headlines symbolized the world tempest in which we were caught?

Every headline of *Communist* (even if that Communist was in Indo-China), every headline of *Investigation* (even if that investigation was in Washington), every headline of *Disloyalty* (even if that disloyalty existed only in some vicious imagination)—every such headline meant that a state of mind was induced and then transferred to the next headline, which read, *U.C. Oath Controversy*. These were the whirlwinds of struggles for world mastery and graspings for power. Yet education—in a democracy—should not be the servant of power.

Nevertheless, as we look at the matter now, with even a little perspective, it seems that the greatest mistake of the regents was not, actually, their lack of trust in the faculty. They made an even more primary error in failing to trust the people of the state.

Facing a fundamental issue, they tried to meet it at a superficial level. Granting that they honestly tried to save something good, the political independence of the University, they tried to do so by instituting something bad, the oath.

Thus they missed a great opportunity. If it had been necessary to fight an adverse constitutional amendment, the regents could have rallied the faculty to a man, and regents, faculty, and alumni together could have met the issue squarely and almost certainly have carried an election. The campaign could, at once, have clearly shown the faculty's loyalty and the competence of the University to be still entrusted with the independence which the Founding Fathers had bestowed upon it so confidently.

Perhaps the people would have decided against us, but the chance would have been worth taking, and the educational value of such a campaign would have been immense. During more than a generation no issue concerning the University has been carried directly to the people. Here was a golden opportunity. Instead of daring our opponents to make the test, thereby insuring themselves of enthusiastic and determined faculty and alumni support, the tragic error of the regents was to choose a way that split the University wide open and unjustly vilified it before the public.

Part Two: Results

CHAPTER 7

The Damage

The purpose of this chapter is to discuss, from what may be called the administrative point of view, the results of the oath controversy; that is, we postpone to the following chapter the delicate psychological problems, and here consider such more tangible matters as changes in personnel.

We have been rash enough to entitle this chapter "The Damage," thus implying that there have been no good results, and would have been no good results even if the requirement of the oath had not been rescinded. This may be argued. Mr. Fox is no longer a T.A., and Mrs. Sherman is no longer with us, and many people certainly believe that the University is better for their absence. Come to think of it, Regent Giannini is no longer with us, either. . . . Well, perhaps our chapter title is not wholly accurate. On the whole, however, it would be difficult to show that good teachers and students have been attracted to the University, or have been kept from leaving it, because of the controversy.

On the other hand, the actual damage, though admittedly great, is difficult to assay. We find the whole inquiry breaking down into three questions. What would have happened if the requirement had not been rescinded? What has happened? What is going to happen? As to the first and third of these, there must obviously be at the present time a large amount of uncertainty; even for the second, statistics are lacking. A

Committee on Academic Freedom has been appointed to investigate, but has not reported.

We therefore, partly from necessity, partly as a literary device, introduce Professor Doe of our Department of Xology. He will present what may be called a departmental case history in the form of an interview.

You may picture Professor Doe as one of our elder statesmen. He wears the slack coat and not-too-well-pressed gray flannels that nowadays constitute the uniform of his profession. He probably smokes his pipe and takes it from between his teeth to hold in his hand judiciously as he answers. You would not, of course, expect him to talk brilliantly. Occasionally, we will admit, he even sounds like the *New Yorker* cliché expert, but that is doubtless to some extent the influence of the interview form itself. In any case, we rather like Professor Doe. He seems well informed about his department, though he is not its chairman. He knows something about the younger men, who are to make the future of the department. Whether he would have been a die-hard non-signer we have no idea, but he is a good, solid faculty man, and we are sure that, even if he had felt compelled to sign, he would have done so with the greatest reluctance.

But remember—though we are pleased to describe the professor thus facetiously—this department is a real one, actually existing upon one of the campuses of the University. There is no real fiction in what he tells us.

A DEPARTMENTAL CASE HISTORY

QUESTION: Professor Doe, will you kindly tell us a little about your department?

ANSWER: The department is a large one, with more than thirty Senate members. I believe that it would certainly rank as one of the best half dozen departments of Xology in the country, perhaps in the top three.

Q: Has it in recent years been a well-functioning, a "happy" department?

A: Yes, in spite of some personal antipathies and some fights over policy, I believe that I can say so.

Q: Do you consider yourself competent to testify as to what would have happened to your department if the special oath had not been rescinded?

A: I do. . . . Of course, "what would have happened" involves a hypothetical element. But I have been closely in touch with the situation in our department all through the year.

Q: How many members of your department would have been dismissed for failure to sign the oath?

A: Six.

Q: Their ranks?

A: Three professors, one associate professor, two assistant professors. This would have been nearly one fifth of the department.

Q: Would you say that this figure is a minimal one, or does it represent the greatest possible number?

A: Most certainly it is minimal. I am convinced that these men would not have signed. If any mass movement toward resignation had developed, as seemed likely at various times, a much larger number of our members would have left the University. Quite possibly as many as half of them would have joined such a movement and faced dismissal. Perhaps I should also add that shortly before April 21 two of the influential members of the department started a strong "Stay, sign, and fight!" program. As a result of this several of our men may have refrained from taking the most extreme position. Moreover, a few of our members began to work on the project of preparing this book, and the chance thus given them actually to carry on the fight would have had some influence in allowing them conscientiously to sign the oath on the assurance that they could still continue to resist what lay behind the imposition of the oath.

Q: Would there have been any other damage?

A: Certainly. Some of our assistant professors and instructors with young families felt that they were forced to take the oath by economic pressure. They would, however, immediately have set about getting other jobs, and since they are excellent youngsters, they would have been able to do so. I estimate that by June 1951 five more members of the department, chiefly younger men, would have found other jobs.

Q: Would you say that the department would then have been faced with a serious situation?

A: If I am correct, by June 1951 we would have lost about one third of our present staff and the work of the department would have been crippled.

Q: In such a situation, would you have had difficulty in recruiting the department?

A: Most certainly! As I often said in those days, "If I sign the oath, I can still teach my classes and I can even do my research. What I do not see is how I can aid in the recruiting of the department. I cannot conscientiously ask other men to come here. If the University extends an invitation to some man, and if he writes me to know whether he should come, I shall be forced to write to him that I believe he should not come."

Q: During the course of the year, did you have an actual indication that recruiting would become difficult?

A: Yes. We had extended an invitation to one of the most distinguished Xologists in the country. He was considering it seriously. After the regents' ultimatum, however, he rejected the offer, and I believe that he wrote a very indignant letter about it.

Q: Would any other difficulties have resulted?

A: Yes, before April 21 we had already had difficulty with our summer-session appointments. One prominent professor whom we had invited from the East wrote that he would certainly not come if the requirement of the oath was not rescinded. We would have found it difficult to fill the vacancy.

Q. Would not one of your own people have filled in, in the emergency?

A: That is doubtful. They would have tended to regard it as "scabbing."

Q: Is there any other indication that this matter of "scabbing" would have caused difficulties?

A: I can illustrate with an anecdote. Some time ago one of our instructors came to me and said, in effect: "Professor N—— has said he is not going to sign the oath. He is in the same field as I am in. If he is dismissed, I do not think that I should take over the courses which he has traditionally given in the department."

Q: Now that the oath has been rescinded, what is the situation?

A: Six of our members—though not in every instance the same ones who refused to sign the oath—have refused to sign the whole contract and are therefore going before the Committee on Privilege and Tenure for investigation.

Q: Do you believe that any of these men will be dismissed?

A: No. I do not believe that any one of them is a Communist, and I assume that that fact will be demonstrated.

Q: In that case will everything be as it was a year or two ago?

A. No. I do not know, for instance, that the professor whom we have invited would reconsider and come to us now, under the circumstances. You must remember that he already has a good job. I think it possible, moreover, that we shall find our younger men drifting away. If one of them should get an offer, we older men might not feel that we could conscientiously urge him very hard to stay here. The situation is still, to say the least, uncertain. Until our faculty has been able to re-establish its position with respect to the regents, we shall have neither the confidence nor the pride that we had a year ago, and we shall have a corresponding difficulty in recruiting and holding our staff.

A question naturally to be asked is, "How typical is Professor Doe's department?" In most respects we have no hesitation in saying it is typical. Probably, however, its number of die-hard non-signers and of non-signers of the contract is higher than average. By a little figuring we arrive at the interesting conclusion that if the same rate of non-signers had held throughout the University, approximately three hundred members of the Senate would have been dismissed on April

30. Somewhat more than two hundred of these would have been of the Northern Section, somewhat fewer than one hundred of the smaller Southern Section.

This is considerably higher than most people think the number would have been. Yet it is difficult to be sure. There were the so-called "breast-beating non-signers," who arose in the Senate and elsewhere and declared that they would never, never sign. We believe that they would not have signed. There were also the "non-breast-beating non-signers." These were the quiet fellows who said little or nothing but went their own ways. We do not know how many of them there were, and we never shall know. There may have been, Professor Doe privately admits, some of these even in his department that he did not know about. One of the six whom he lists he discovered only at the last moment, almost by accident, although he knew the man well. That particular professor was simply not talking.

Certainly, however, the Department of Xology was not the extreme in either direction. Of one department—and not a small one—it had been consistently reported from the beginning that they would all leave. Another department, somewhat smaller, would probably have lost more than half its members. A third department, small but highly distinguished, would have lost about half. Another large department would have lost heavily, and even as the situation now stands it is losing one of its most brilliant young men, who refuses to stay with the University any longer.

For still another large department we have statistics supplied by the chairman, who himself would not have signed. This department has about twenty-five Senate members. According to the well-considered judgment of its chairman, the losses would have been: five professors; one associate professor; two assistant professors. This would have constituted approximately one third of the Senate members. In addition, the department would have lost one lecturer and five teaching assistants. With so many professors leaving, some graduate students had also expressed their intention of leaving, since they could not work without proper instruction and supervision.

On the other hand, many departments would have lost but slightly, and three from which we have collected the probable statistics would have lost no one at all, at least of Senate rank.

As to how great the drift away from the University would have been after April 30 and how great the difficulty of recruiting would have been, we are inclined to think that Professor Doe expresses the situation well enough. Definite plans were actually being laid in certain quarters, not only not to call men to fill the vacant places, but even to resist efforts by the administration to fill those places, by warning the academic world in general that any professor coming to the University without the invitation of his fellow professors could expect only minimal professional co-operation· and would remain socially ostracized. Even among those who would have had to sign and stay, the fighting spirit was not broken. They would have remained good Americans, resolved still to maintain the struggle for the restoration of their professional and personal liberties.

CHAPTER 8

Life in the Ivory Tower

Where a tribe of professors now inhabits the Faculty Club on the Berkeley campus there was once the camp site of a tribe of Costanoans. Under the northeast corner of the present building, anthropologists have discovered graves and skeletons of the former inhabitants.

This particular tribe vanished long ago, but we can assume that they were like the others of the region. If so, they lived in a secure and benevolent environment, rich in acorns, quail, and rabbits. They were not warlike. In the ordinary course of life, leisurely tribal decisions could be made after long conversations at the sweat-house, that lodge which served as sudatory and dormitory and men's meeting place, thus being not altogether unlike a Faculty Club.

At last came the sudden encroachment of Spaniards, all-powerful with horses, arrow-stopping armor, and firearms.

Then must have come frantic and despairing council in the sweat-house. Doubtless these Costanoans were as brave as any other men, as well fitted to manage their ordinary problems of life. Doubtless some of them, uncompromising, counseled resistance, and others pointed out that resistance against such power was mere suicide. Doubtless some advised flight; others, abject submission. If the period of strain was long extended, and the recorded history of other tribes offers analogy, we may believe that the individual tribesmen suffered psychologically. When the bravest were daunted and the wisest were confused, when the most active found nothing purposive to do, we can only believe that many tribesmen became acutely depressed, that old friends quarreled, that certain renegades went over to the enemy, and that a kind of general disintegration set in. . . . Such a fate also threatened the tribe of professors.

The faculty of a large state university is not, indeed, a distinct tribe. It is, in fact, highly representative of the general population, almost a cross section. Its members are drawn from various regions of the country, come from diverse backgrounds, follow widely differing interests, and manifest much the same range of political opinion and social outlook as might be expected from any non-academic group. Nevertheless, a faculty is like a primitive tribe in that it is fairly close knit, earns its livelihood by the same means, inhabits the same environment, and bases its life upon certain established *mores*.

We must remember also that this particular faculty consisted almost wholly of native Americans and thus possessed both the strengths and the weaknesses that an anthropologist sees in our national character. From earliest childhood they had been reared in the tradition of independence, activity, and initiative. During the Year of the Oath, however, the ordinary faculty member, unless he was not serving on a committee, felt himself being shoved around, and yet could do nothing about it, except occasionally to shout "Aye!" with the rest of the Senate. Take away initiative from an American, and he has little to fall back on. He feels frustrated and begins to suffer psychologically.

A faculty, moreover, contains a high proportion of men and women trained to examine the consequences of ideas and professionally accustomed to tracing the implications of seemingly trivial acts. In a faculty, also, are a very large number of highly organized and sensitive people. Many of these are artists—architects, musicians, writers, painters. Research workers, also, are essentially creative and have much in common with artists, and so do good teachers.

All such people felt the strain of the Year of the Oath. The threat to the University, therefore, cannot be judged entirely in what may be called administrative terms (see Chapter 7) but also must be considered in terms of actual damage to the individual. Toward the end of the year the expression, "Life in the Ivory Tower," came to be used with ironic significance, as indicating not an existence withdrawn from the world, but one in which the individual was exposed to more than the usual harassments and frustrations.

To find out what had actually happened we made use of two methods. A questionnaire was prepared by several faculty members with professional competency in the polling field and was sent to every fourth name in the directory of the Berkeley faculty. In addition, a group of the faculty members, most of whom used interviewing techniques professionally, conducted a series of forty-two interviews. The questionnaire was designed to provide some general and quantitative appraisal. The interviews went more deeply into the problems of a comparatively small number of individuals.

Over the signature of the chief author, with the statement that the material would be used in the preparation of this book, 302 questionnaires were sent out on May 8, 1950. The date is of significance because the faculty went into a bad slump after the release from the highest period of tension in the weeks preceding April 21. The questionnaire, therefore, by accident and not design, probably recorded a maximum disturbance.

One questionnaire was returned personally with the statement that it was "too dangerous" to be involved with. Two people wrote letters saying that they did not believe the project to be in the best interests of the University. Three others wrote letters indicating that, for various reasons, they were not returning the questionnaire. In time for compilation, 174 questionnaires were returned. Of these, 28 per cent came from non-signers of the oath, 69 per cent from signers, and 3 per cent from individuals who failed to state. Since only about 20 per cent of the Berkeley faculty were non-signers, the greater percentage returning questionnaires indicates their more intense interest in the oath controversy, and also undoubtedly results in a slight skewing of the questionnaire in the non-signer direction.

The answers show a wide spread of opinion and emphasize the fact, already mentioned elsewhere, that one can scarcely write of "*the* faculty point of view." Nevertheless, there are significant clusterings of response under nearly every heading.

The first question asked: "When you think back over the entire situation, what would you say was the most significant effect that the oath controversy had on you personally?" Interestingly, 3 per cent considered the effects to be beneficial because of the increased faculty solidarity. Only 8 per cent indicated that they had felt little or no effect. The rest (89 per cent) attested to strong deleterious effects. Of these, 28 per cent expressed themselves as chiefly concerned about such matters as the anti-democratic threat that they believed to be involved in the requirements of the oath. They expressed fears about the growth of Fascism, the police state, and the loss of civil liberties. Loss of confidence in the faculty, in the regents, and in the president was indicated, respectively, by 25 per cent, 12 per cent, and 11 per cent. (These figures do not mean, of course, that more people lost confidence in the faculty than in the regents, but only that, by the proportions indicated, they rated this loss of confidence as the *most important* effect upon them personally.) Interpreting the question subjectively, 11 per cent indicated such personal problems as worry, depression, fatigue, fear, insomnia, drinking, headaches, and indigestion. The other answers were scattering.[1]

As to the degree of personal involvement in the situation, 40 per cent answered "very preoccupied," 40 per cent "moderately," and 20 per cent "very little."

To the question, "Were your personal relations with other members of the faculty impaired during the period of the oath controversy?" "Yes" answers totaled 23 per cent; "No" answers, 75 per cent. (General awareness of the situation, however, suggests that there was more disruption in faculty

[1]From other sources we record two known cases of ulcers and several instances of strained marital relations. At a large hospital patronized by faculty members a nurse was heard to remark, "Oh, we've had lots of oath cases!"

relations than the figures would here indicate, and that the comparatively low figure springs from unconscious resistance on the part of the individuals toward admitting that their personal relationships with their colleagues had suffered.) Of those who admitted such disruptions, 5 per cent mentioned actual quarrels; 3 per cent, the breaking of specific friendships. Curiously, 23 per cent expressed loss of respect for their colleagues, but only 10 per cent indicated a fear that they themselves had lost their colleagues' respect! Conflicts developing from differences of opinion were mentioned by 32 per cent; a general growth of suspicion and distrust in the faculty, by 25 per cent.

Nearly all (87 per cent) felt that at some time during the year the University "was endangered." Of these, 64 per cent felt that it was still endangered after the compromise of April 21, and 32 per cent that it was still possibly endangered. As to *why* the University was still endangered, 43 per cent of those who thought so attributed their fear to the loss of Academic Freedom and faculty autonomy. On the other hand, 3 per cent thought that the extremists among the non-signers would keep the issue alive and that there would be Communist infiltration into the faculty. Other significant groups indicated lack of confidence in the compromise (30 per cent), loss of public support because of bad publicity (11 per cent), and loss of prestige in the eyes of the academic world (34 per cent).

To the question, "Would you now be more receptive to a reasonable offer from another university than you were before the oath controversy began?" the answers were "Yes, definitely," 38 per cent; "Might be," 22 per cent; "No," 35 per cent.

As to whether the new contract would be an effective means of excluding members of the Communist Party from the faculty, the answers were: "Yes," 11 per cent; "No," 73 per cent; "Don't know," 16 per cent.

Lack of confidence in the compromise also came out in replies to the question, "Do you think it likely that the present procedure will jeopardize the employment of some non-Communist members of the faculty?" To this, 60 per cent answered "Likely"; 22 per cent, "Not likely," and 17 per cent admitted, "Don't know."

To the very significant question, "On the whole, are you proud of the way the faculty has conducted itself?" only 30 per cent answered "Yes," and 65 per cent "No." Of those who answered "No," 14 per cent thought that opposition to the oath had been too strong, 55 per cent that opposition had been not strong enough, and 31 per cent specified more particular reasons.

The forty-two interviews also were of great importance in assaying the results of the oath upon the collective faculty personality. The interviewers made their selections from widely varying types and included representatives of various departments and of more than one campus, of all academic ranks, and of signers and non-signers. The interviews were then roughly classified. Seven interesting and significant ones are here condensed and presented as case histories. All pronouns have been rendered in the masculine, and other means of identification have been removed. There has been an attempt, however, to render feeling tone by preservation of the individual's particular vocabulary.

1

One of the characteristic responses throughout the first part of the controversy was the feeling in the faculty ranks of a satisfaction at unity, of exhilaration, almost of exaltation. For a few fortunate individuals some remnants of this early happiness remained even through the darkest weeks.

PROFESSOR A (Assistant Professor, Letters and Science, two years' service.)

Mr. A's first response was one of great satisfaction with his colleagues. He came away from the Senate meeting of June 14 "with a lump in the throat," proud that he belonged to the University, and confident that a group with such principles and determination would win. These feelings persisted for a long time and were nourished by successive Senate meetings, each dispelling for a while the doubt and insecurity that the ever-worsening situation induced. During the summer he was pleased that a friend from the East was visiting the University, and hoped that his friend could be induced to join so fine a faculty after seeing what a determined fight it was putting up.

By March his optimism was gone, but he was still warmed by the personal sympathy of a small group of his colleagues, some of them older men, and by the determination of the non-signers' group of which he remained a member. He still feels that adversity has made him firmer in his position, that as the group has become smaller he has had increasingly greater confidence in its members, and he thinks that he has found some permanent friends among them.

2

Throughout the summer and fall there was mounting anxiety. Especially among younger faculty members, feelings of insecurity developed. Signers developed feelings of guilt toward non-signers. Reluctant signers joined with non-signers in suspicion of the relatively few signers who favored the oath.

PROFESSOR B (Associate Professor, Letters and Science, fourteen years' service.)

When the content of the oath was announced, Mr. B became indignant and did not want to sign if he could avoid it. His indignation at the oath as a political test caused him the most disturbance, but in August he became even angrier than before at not getting his contract, and became very angry at the president and the regents. Being worried also, he went to the President's Office and the Regents' Office and could not find out whether he would be paid or not, but the implication was that he would not be. He became frightened. (Mr. B has heavy family responsibilities and is making payments on a house.) Believing that he would probably not be paid, he signed on September 29.

He has felt steadily "madder" and has felt an increasing desire to fight, but also an increasing futility. He finds himself always explaining why he had to sign, and feels guilty. He notices the same reaction in other signers and the sense of insecurity among his friends, particularly among those who are non-signers.

He thinks that the University business office is keeping tab on faculty members' activities, both within and without the University.

He is gloomy for the future, thinks the worst is yet to come. The University's reputation will be bad and it will be hard to bring able people to the faculty. Thinks it would be a good idea to try to get an offer elsewhere. He would rather be here, but this all makes him think of getting away.

He has the feeling of successive defeats. Each regents' meeting, when he felt things might be better, resulted in things getting worse. Although he has felt hopeless from the first, and still has the same feeling of hopelessness, he seems surprised to find that he feels so gloomy about it all.

3

Among the non-signers there was a good deal of understandable anxiety, insecurity, and even fear, though they were courageously putting themselves into an exposed position. They were acting from principle, but their attitude in the periods of greatest tension was often not so much moral exaltation as desperation. They felt bitter against their colleagues for "letting them down" and felt that their colleagues should be protecting them.

PROFESSOR C (Assistant Professor, Agriculture, ten years' service.)

He has been afraid of the consequences ever since he refused to sign at the beginning, and doesn't really understand why he hasn't signed yet. Has waited from deadline to dead-line and taken one alternative after another, hoping for a satisfactory way out. He described it as "a feeling of being trapped and not knowing whether I was a mouse or a lion." He has been afraid to face his wife with the alternative of unemployment, but he still cannot sign. He resents having been put into this dilemma and hopes that older men will somehow rule him out of the controversy or protect him in some way. He is not typical of his department, which has been relatively unmoved by the whole thing. Has not suffered in his department in terms of human relations, but he feels that he is not so brave as younger colleagues think him, and not so foolish as older ones think him. (His total attitude is one of nervousness and indecision, of apprehension for the future, and particularly of confusion as to his own nature and motives.)

4

Early in May the situation was one of almost complete depression and gloom for many people. Furthermore, it had become apparent that, although some of the gloom would pass, some of the damage had been permanent.

PROFESSOR D (Professor, Letters and Science, twelve years' service.)

Professor D thinks that the faculty now can be divided into non-signers, either because of principles or because of their interest in the struggle for power; second, those who sign but have a bad conscience and are sympathetic to non-signers; third, those who have signed and are vicious about it, who would like to fire non-signers and dislike them; and fourthly, conservatives who tend to bend too far in compromise and have difficulty in understanding non-signers. Among these groups there exists suspicion, antagonism, irritability, defen-siveness, and aggressiveness.

As for the events of the next two years, this professor

thinks that that depends on what the regents do. If they do not fire anyone except on definite proof of Communism, he thinks things will calm down. "Still so much harm has already been done to morale, and personal frictions have so developed, that the wounds will take time to heal, regardless of the outcome. Some wounds will never be healed." He feels that the faculty has been subjected to fear and the sense of insecurity as no human being should be subjected. He is depressed. He is disgusted that a university of this greatness and size should be involved in a conflict so thoroughly rooted in mass hysteria. For himself, he is in a state of exhaustion and suffers from insomnia, and his family, he says, is exhausted too. And yet he is determined not to give in to pressure, and he sees on the positive side the fact that working with others gives him a kind of minimum security which enables him to stick it out. Since basic issues, he says, in critical times seem always to concern the responsibility of a minority group, he has the feeling of engaging in a rewarding battle in terms of principle and in terms of building up a safer environment for himself and his children. On the other hand, he is bitter that all this should have to happen in a country as strong as the United States.

5

Especially in April and May, depression became common. It displayed the two recognized forms—the apathetic and the agitated. While in either condition, the individual failed to function well. In the belief that all these men were essentially sound, several of them were enlisted in work on this book. Some of them, but not all, recovered immediately with the opportunity for purposive work and became essential workers. They expressed a new interest in life and showed great psychological improvement. A few, who otherwise might not have done so, signed the contract, preferring to remain and work actively, and no longer feeling the same conscientious strain.

In Professor E's interview his depressed feeling tone was marked, along with his pervasive uncertainty. This latter was most acute in relation to the question of what action he would take on the contract.

PROFESSOR E (Associate Professor, Medicine, seven years' service.)

He became aware of the importance of the issue in June 1949. He first said, "June—almost two years ago, wasn't it?" He was incredulous at first that it had been less than a year ago.

In departments where the senior members took a strong stand, he thinks that the morale was high. "Now everything is coming apart. I don't know what to do. I have to decide tonight." He doesn't want to be a martyr. So long as he was one of a hundred or more he felt secure. Now nobody knows how many holdouts there are, nor what support there will be for them. As one of maybe twenty-five, he has no security. Communication is broken down. He keeps fearing that more and more non-signers have decided to sign. "It's the aloneness . . . feeling completely cut off since the last regents' meeting . . . the falling away."

6

The strain spared no age group. Perhaps those of middle years (such as Professor B) were in the worst situation, having heavy family responsibilities and being already at an age when the getting of a new position is not easy. Instructors and assistant professors, not yet well established in the University and better able to get new jobs, were in a slightly less difficult position. So were older professors, within a few years of retirement, although even these were worried that their retiring allowances would not be given them if they were dismissed. Nevertheless, the actual amount of psychic disturbance seems more proportionate to the individual's temperament than to his actual risk. Many older professors who had devoted their lives to the University now felt that their world was going to pieces around them.

Such a one is Professor F, a man with a long and brilliant career behind him, known to all his colleagues for his fighting spirit. This courage did not fail him during the Year of the Oath, but he did not escape without suffering.

PROFESSOR F (Professor, Letters and Science, thirty-five years' service.)

He has lost his zest for teaching and has been ashamed to find himself looking forward to freedom from teaching. He feels that, having signed, he could not face his students and teach. Has found it nearly impossible to work during the past year; there has been none of the peace of mind necessary for intellectual pursuits either as teacher or as scholar. He has lost sleep and appetite; after attending meetings of non-signers he was unable to sleep at all unless he took sedatives. Feels that his health has been definitely affected. Has been completely preoccupied with controversy to the exclusion of any other thought or interest. Feels that there is a tragedy of imminent disintegration of the University. Is disappointed in people who have been his friends for years, particularly in some committee members and in the stool pigeons.

If he finds his friends disagreeing with him violently, he no longer wants to see them and has withdrawn from the association with many of his oldest friends. Has always felt a tremendous need to be tolerant of other people's opinions; has often disagreed with good friends and still respected them, but is now afraid to be tolerant. Cannot trust the judgment of others who do not feel as he does about this. Within his own department, feels that the bitterness of the controversy has wrecked the morale of the whole group. Has found it heartening that so many wives of non-signers feel as strongly as their husbands. Has been encouraged because so many of the non-signers are younger men with a great deal to lose, but still willing to risk everything because of principles.

In spite of his firm attitude, he said suddenly, "I'm afraid!"

Nevertheless, he declares that he did not sign the oath and will not sign the contract.

7

In contrast, there was a considerable group of faculty members who remained quite undisturbed. On the questionnaire one of these replied to the question as to his state of mind by the single word "Placid."

PROFESSOR G (Associate Professor, Letters and Science, ten years' service.)

He characterizes the whole controversy as "much ado about nothing." Considers it a tremendous, lamentable waste of time, used by many of the faculty as an excuse not to work, as an evasion of other and more important responsibilities. Has been a non-participant in the controversy at all its stages.

With Professor G our list of seven interviews comes to an end. Some representative from another (small but interesting) group of professors should have been included in this chapter, but an approach to any of them seemed scarcely practicable.

During the course of the controversy members of faculty committees became aware that what had happened in closed meetings of the Senate and even in smaller faculty groups was immediately known to certain of the regents. An inference was soon inescapable. Although conscientious members of the faculty were prevented by one of the Standing Orders from approaching a regent directly, this order did not prevent less conscientious members of the faculty from carrying information to certain regents, who did not feel themselves restrained by their own order. To discover who these agents might be, it is rumored that certain former OSS men assumed the old cloak and dagger once more and renewed their wartime proficiency in counterespionage. Before long, on the Berkeley campus, the names of three such men were known for certain, and they were thenceforth called "The Black Triumvirate," or more colloquially, "those——stool pigeons!" Similar discoveries were made in Los Angeles.

In addition to the undercover workers, a certain less objectionable type of professor espoused the anti-Senate position publicly, allowed himself to be quoted in the press, or wrote letters to regents, which were in turn printed. Probably nothing was more enraging to other faculty members, and more damaging to the morale of such men, than the discovery of these two kinds of defection.

We may spare space for two anecdotes. . . . Publicly a professor of the second group was heard to declare loudly: "I have no respect for the Academic Senate!" Whereupon a colleague replied: "The feeling, sir, is mutual!"

On another campus one professor remarked: "Isn't it terrible we're finding out that we can't trust some of our colleagues!" The reply was: "Not at all! The b——ds were there all the time; now we know who they are!"

Along with such discoveries went a steadily mounting sense of personal insecurity, suspicion, and fear, verging into paranoia. Some active non-signers came to believe—and still believe—that their telephones were tapped. Even more common was the belief that the University telephones, at least those of committee members, were in some way monitored at the switchboard. So common was this belief that, when work on this book was begun, use of the University telephones was found to be impractical because a considerable number of people flatly refused to discuss anything important over those lines.

Other professors reported strangers visiting their classes, apparently taking notes on what was said. Such incidents were removed from the realm of the wholly fanciful when two agents of a dean were definitely located and identified as taking down names at a meeting of the Non-Senate Academic Employees.

One eminent professor, a non-signer, looked into his memory and recalled that several years previous, with the consent of his chairman, he had committed a small infringement of a University regulation, a matter little more important than parking in front of a campus fire hydrant. He became convinced that, even if he escaped disaster over the oath, this ancient peccadillo would be raked up and cause his dismissal.

There is no need to go farther into this sad phase of the affair. The main trouble is actually to decide whether we are dealing with paranoia or with actuality. So many incredible things happened on our campuses during the Year of the Oath that we are scarcely ready to maintain that any particular kind of thing did not happen. As one man remarked when asked if he had had any suspicions: "Well, I don't know whether you'd call them suspicions or not. They all turned out to be true!" The professor mentioned in the preceding paragraph has not yet been dismissed because of his small error. But who are we to say that he may not be? . . .

We should emphasize again that the date of the questionnaires and interviews (early May) is important in that at that time the faculty was at a low point. There is little reason to think that the damage inflicted by the strain of the year will in many cases be permanent.

Anyone may also question, when all is said and done, whether the reactions here recorded are particularly characteristic of a faculty group or whether similar actions might not also be recorded in any group of human beings after a period of strain. If a similar study should be made in the ranks of a labor union at the end of a prolonged and desperate strike, we might well expect the same results.[2]

---

[2]Before being put into final form this chapter was read by a specialist in the dynamics of society from the psychoanalytic point of view, himself a professor and a non-signer of both oath and contract. He approved the general interpretation offered in the chapter, and the particular analogies of the Indian tribe and the labor union. In addition we reproduce a few notes taken down roughly from his conversation: "Neuroticism, as here, is likely to set in, when the community is not backing up the individual so that the individual loses the sense of identity that he usually gets from his job. . . . Changes in historical forces give people a sense that the methods by which they have mastered the environment are put out of commission. Insecurity results. The professors had great confidence in individual judgment, and as researchers and teachers had based their lives on it. They were

The writer of this chapter, by the chance of random sampling, happened to be one of those to receive the questionnaire. To the question, "On the whole, are you proud of the way the faculty has conducted itself?" he answered "Yes." Although by the results of the questionnaire he finds himself put into a minority of one to two, he still maintains his position. To support himself, moreover, he would argue that in the last two months he has spent a great deal of time studying the matter, has had a very large number of facts placed at his disposal, and has been forced—as a writer—to view the facts with a considerable degree of objectivity.

There is no space here for much arguing, nor does the writer feel that, merely because he happens to be such, he should express his own ideas at great length. Nevertheless, as the result of a fuller study of the questionnaire than it has here been possible to present, and as a result of study of all forty-two interviews, the writer may be allowed a personal comment.

The faculty has been accused of cowardice. Fear there certainly was, and there was some yielding to it. "He jests at scars that never felt a wound." There was also an amazing display of courage, at many times and by many individuals, in the faculty ranks.

The faculty has been accused of neuroticism. Some of the case histories here presented would certainly lend authority to that statement. Actually, however, there is no evidence that an equal amount of neuroticism might not be discovered in any other group under similar circumstances.

We should always remember, moreover, that the damage which these highly sensitive men and women foresaw, and the danger to which they reacted, was not primarily in their

---

suddenly subjected to mass pressure, and raw power began to steam-roller them. We may say that they came up against the machine age. . . . The faculty tried to stick by its ideals; the only way to have won the immediate decisions would have been to become wholly cynical. . . . Frustrations develop with the sense that life is not worth living, and this develops when the community seems to have lost confidence in the job you are doing."

minds a disaster or a menace to a particular person or even to their whole group. From the evidence of the questionnaires and of the interviews we see that it was rather conceived as the menace to the ideal of the University, as a threat to free teaching and learning, as an undermining of that independence of thought so vital, not only to the academic way of life, but also, especially in this time of universal stress, to the whole world.

Part Three: Larger Aspects

CHAPTER 9

"You Too Can Have a Loyalty Oath!"

During a recent hilarious demonstration at one of our sister universities, students carried banners exhorting their faculty to greater efforts. One of these read: "You too can be a great university! You too can have a loyalty oath!" There is, unfortunately, too much sober truth in the second part of this slogan. . . .

During the year, professors of the University of California were frequently humiliated by the complacent and condescending manner of professors from other institutions, especially of private ones, who seemed to assume that the trouble about the oath must spring from some inherent rottenness at the University of California, perhaps from some secret sin in which its professors had previously indulged.

Yes, perhaps we had sinned. Pride is held to be a deadly sin, and before this year we had felt great pride in our University and in being part of it. Perhaps, to our shame, we had looked on complacently, and even spoken condescendingly, when other faculties got into trouble.

As we see the matter now, however, we believe that nothing in the system of control or in the tradition of an American college or university is an absolute guarantee that its Academic Freedom will not be impaired. At best, all any professor can say is, "It hasn't happened here!" To be safe, he had better say, "It hasn't happened here *yet!*" He should never say, "It can't happen here!"

To present evidence on this point we summarize some cases, taken from the *Bulletin* of the American Association of University Professors. These range in time from 1915 to 1944. In most of them the president of the institution was allied with the Board; in a few notable instances, with the accused professor or professors. As elsewhere in this book, however, the focus of attention is not upon the president but upon the Board.

Each of these cases has been carefully investigated by the A.A.U.P. In each the investigating committee disapproved, in one way or another, usually in strong terms, of the action of the Board. To avoid a monotonous refrain, we omit some of these comments.

The cases here presented are only a selection. Many others might be added from the files of the *Bulletin*. Moreover, the great majority of such incidents probably escape observation entirely. Most cases of infringement of Academic Freedom probably come to light only because of what might be called inept administration. In the others, the "offender" is disciplined "through regular channels" and with proper protocol—merely for supposed lack of the qualities necessary for his position.

Moreover, it should be strongly emphasized that in the cases here presented the professor stood his ground and refused to yield to pressure. There is no catalogue of the certainly much more numerous instances in which a professor, caught by economic pressure, yielded to more or less politely veiled threats, probably channeled to him through the president and the head of his department, and ceased to discuss "dangerous" doctrines in his classes or otherwise knuckled under.

None of the cases here presented is exactly analogous to our own. Point-to-point similarity is hardly to be expected. Nevertheless, we believe they all represent the same fundamental problem; that is, the interference of a non-professional board with Academic Tenure, and thus necessarily with Academic Freedom.

UNIVERSITY OF PENNSYLVANIA

On June 14, 1915, Scott Nearing, assistant professor of economics in the Wharton School, was denied reappointment by the Board of Trustees who thus refused to accept the recommendation of the dean of the school. Influential alumni, with whom one trustee joined, had been campaigning actively against Nearing because of his "radical teachings." They maintained that only "sound" economic doctrines (i.e., substantially those held by Joseph Wharton, the school's founder) should be taught, and that professors should not express themselves on controversial social questions in the classroom or in public statements outside the University. The A.A.U.P. committee found that Nearing had been summarily dismissed because of his convictions and in spite of his colleagues' wishes.

WOOSTER COLLEGE

In April 1916, Winona Hughes, dean of women, was dismissed. The situation was complicated. It involved, along with much else, a fight on Dean Hughes's part against low academic standards. The A.A.U.P. committee decided that the president and certain trustees compassed the dismissal of Dean Hughes without just cause and in a manner wholly at variance with proper standards.

MONTANA STATE UNIVERSITY

This institution has been a chronic offender. It is governed by a State Board of Education, but this Board differs little in its composition from the ordinary board of regents. On June 7–8, 1915, the Board dismissed President E. B. Craighead, Professors G. F. Reynolds and T. L. Bolton, and Dean Mary Stewart. President Craighead was dismissed because of his opposition to certain policies of the Board. Curiously, the two professors and the dean were opponents of the president's stand and were dismissed in order to placate the minority of the Board who favored the president. They were discharged at the end of the academic year without notice, without charges, without a hearing, without the recommendation of any responsible faculty agency.

THE SAME

In 1919 the chancellor suspended Louis Levine, professor of economics, for having privately published a monograph on mine taxation which was displeasing to certain powerful interests in the state. By a curious action, the Board, though reinstating Levine after a review of his case, voted to approve the chancellor's action in suspending him.

THE SAME

On April 12, 1937, the Board placed J. P. Rowe, professor of geology, on month-to-month tenure and supported the decision of the president not to reappoint the librarian, Professor Philip Keeney. Rowe, together with a majority of the faculty, had opposed the appointment of President G. F. Simmons and was disciplined for his supposed antagonism to the administration. No evidence of obstructionist tactics on Rowe's part was proved. Keeney had also been the president's opponent and had been outspoken against censorship of library books by the Board or the president. A member of the Board charged him with advocating "socialistic, communistic, and atheistic attitudes" and with "vulgar discussion of sex matters" in his classes.

THE SAME

In 1937, Professor Paul C. Phillips, head of the Department of History and vice-president of the University, resigned his appointment because his involvement as the defendant in a court action had placed him in an ambiguous position in the University. He resigned with the understanding that if he was cleared he would be reinstated. Dr. Phillips won his case and was further cleared of charges against him by a faculty committee. Nevertheless, President Simmons refused to recommend his reinstatement to the University. The A.A.U.P. committee suggested that there was an undue influence exercised over University affairs by Missoula business interests, that President Simmons owed his appointment as president to that group, and that Dr. Phillips was *persona non grata* to that group.

UNIVERSITY OF MISSOURI

On April 6–7, 1929, the Board of Curators voted to suspend Professor M. F. Meyer (social psychology) for one year without pay and to dismiss Professor H. O. De Graff (sociology), both sentences to take effect on April 8. De Graff was dismissed without pay for the remainder of the academic year. These professors had permitted the circulation, in one of De Graff's classes, of a questionnaire on sex and family problems. The president, some of the curators, and some townspeople were shocked. (Who is this man Kinsey?) The A.A.U.P. committee reported: "By [its] action, the Board of Curators served notice on the faculty of the University of Missouri that the Board has and may exercise the right of dismissal of any member of the faculty whose teaching and research does [*sic*] not conform to the undeclared standards of the Board."

OHIO STATE UNIVERSITY

On May 13, 1930, the Board of Trustees voted to give Herbert A. Miller, professor of sociology, a terminal appointment for 1930–31. Some members of the Board did not like his opinions on race relations.

UNIVERSITY OF PITTSBURGH

On June 30, 1934, the chancellor of the University informed Ralph F. Turner, associate professor of history, that his services were then and there terminated, although he would be given one year's salary in place of a terminal appointment. No reasons were given him. Investigation proved that in his classes he discussed evolution, the origins of religious institutions, and controversial political questions. The A.A.U.P. committee found that the chancellor, with the support of the Board, was maintaining a university in which faculty members were seriously intimidated.

WEST CHESTER STATE TEACHERS COLLEGE

Late in the spring in 1938, Mr. H. M. Sherman and Professor J. C. Johnson were notified of the termination of their contracts with the West Chester State Teachers College. Charges against both men were nebulous and seemed to focus on personal antipathy between them and the president. Both men were accused, without clear cause, of disloyalty to the policies of the Board of Trustees, which, in the opinion of the A.A.U.P. committee, meant merely that they failed to submit unquestioningly to the authority of the trustees. The committee noted further the existence of rumors that "undesirable political pressures play an important part in the administration" of the school.

JOHN B. STETSON UNIVERSITY

During March and April 1938, three members of the College of Law at Stetson University, Associate Professor H. S. Jacobs and Professors J. W. Futch and J. A. Carpenter, were notified that their contracts would not be renewed. Charges against the men on grounds of incompetence were,

in the judgment of the A.A.U.P. committee, without founda-
tion. The trustees of the University were notably passive in
the case and appeared out of direct contact with the affairs
of the school. The committee noted, however, that the vice-
president of the Board of Trustees had in 1937 attempted
to sell Professor Jacobs fire insurance for his new home. On
his refusal, the trustee reminded Jacobs that he was his
employer and was responsible for Jacobs's retaining his job.

UNIVERSITY OF TEXAS

Between 1942 and 1944 the regents dismissed several professors and threatened to dismiss others, contrary to the
recommendations of all the responsible administrative officials
from department chairman to president. These professors,
said the regents, were unfit to teach Texas youth because of
their political and educational views. President Homer P.
Rainey had fought the regents in support of his faculty. On
November 1, 1944, the regents voted to dismiss Rainey as of
that day. This situation resembles that at the University of
California in as much as a "loyalty" campaign was involved.
In this instance the regents interpreted loyalty and patriotism
as complete conformity with their own political and social
prejudices. The University of Texas was, roughly speaking,
ruined. We have here an example, though actually a less
extreme one, of what might have happened to the University
of California if the requirement of the oath had not been
rescinded.

The nature of the offenses in these twelve cases calls
for brief comment. Although questions of sex and race occasionally raise their ugly heads, we should conclude that
Academic Freedom is most often in danger when the professor is less conservative economically and politically than
are the regents. This may be considered in part a natural
outgrowth of our times, which have been concerned with
economic and political problems rather than with, let us

say, religious problems. It results, however, even more from the fact that these boards are composed chiefly of businessmen, especially of bankers and lawyers. (See Chapter 12.) If the boards were composed of ministers, as they once largely were, we should expect religious questions to arise more often. If the boards were composed chiefly of members of the Society for Classical Music, we should suspect that cases might arise about professors of music who included works of Stravinsky in the programs of university orchestras or were suspected of being secret admirers of Hindemith.

CHAPTER 10

"This Is the Way It Begins"

European universities, lacking boards of regents, have been correspondingly free from the peculiarly American problem which has formed the subject of the preceding chapter. European professors, however, in two countries which had rejoiced in a long-enduring and strong tradition of universities have known, in the not too distant past, what it was to suffer beneath the imposition of oaths.

Of all the incidents of the Year of the Oath, perhaps none made a more profound impression upon those who experienced it than the speech of a once German scholar in the Senate meeting of June 14 at Berkeley. Speaking as in a strange rhythmical incantation, high-pitched with fervor, his foreign accent now and then making his words scarcely intelligible, he told of the imposition of oaths in the early days of Hitler's power. His theme was always: "This is the way it begins. The first oath is so gentle that one can scarcely notice anything at which to take exception. The next oath is stronger!" The time to resist, he declared, was at the beginning; the oath to refuse to take was the first oath, the little one. True to the convictions that he thus expressed, he remained steadfastly a non-signer.

Under the Nazi regime the first oath, the little one, was required of civil servants, including professors, on December 2, 1933, only ten months after Hitler had seized power. It read: "I swear: I will keep faith to *Volk* and *Vaterland,* honor the Constitution and the laws, and fulfill my official duties conscientiously, so help me God!" A person might have said that he could scarcely see how any patriotic German would mind swearing to such an oath every morning before breakfast.

Thus started, the requirers of oaths closed in, and the second oath was demanded eight months later. In some ways, indeed, this one asked less. The civil servants, including the university professors, were no longer required to honor the Constitution and the laws, although they were still required to fulfill their official duties conscientiously. Instead of swearing to keep faith to *Volk* and *Vaterland,* they were now required to substitute by declaring their allegiance to *"Adolf Hitler, Führer des deutschen Reiches und Volkes."*

This second oath was not to remain a dead letter. We quote a few examples of the invocation of its power. About 1935 a certain teacher in the University of Berlin received a curt letter from the director of administration, without conventional salutation, which read:

I request you to make me a detailed statement as to whether any of your grandparents are Jewish in blood, and if so, which, and whether any of them are Jewish in religion, and if so, which.

This statement is to be given under pain of offending against the Service Oath.

On January 17, 1935, some professors of the University of Berlin received from their rector a letter which warned them against attending the memorial service planned for a certain once anti-Nazi professor. The letter ended: "I must therefore forbid all my subordinates *sworn in* [italics ours] as State officials to participate in the Ceremony."

We find the oath again as the conclusion to a form letter sent by the same rector to his faculty on May 6, 1935. Certain reports of political importance were to be prepared within a week. Failure of professors to do so, the letter concluded, would be construed as "an offense against their Service Oath."

In Italy also the Fascists lined up the professors by imposing an oath. That the world might know how devoted the scholars of Italy were to Fascism, Mussolini issued the Law of August 28, 1931, in which Article 18 required of all university teachers the oath:

I swear to be loyal to the King, to his Royal Successors, and to the Fascist Regime, loyally to observe the statute and the other laws of the State, to fill my office at the university and all other of my academic duties with the intent to train up industrious, upright citizens devoted to their country and the Regime. I swear that I neither belong nor will belong to associations or parties whose activities are not in accord with my official duties.

Of the professors thus required to swear, William Elwin in his *Fascism at Work* (page 140) records:

They only took the oath under coercion, and consider it consequently as null before their own conscience and that of the world. It was exclusively for their daily bread and under threat of losing life and liberty they were forced into taking the oath.

It seems worthy of mention, however, that many of Italy's most illustrious savants had the courage to reply: "No" to the Government.

Among others who refused to take this oath were the former Prime Minister, Vittorio Emanuele Orlando, and Professors Gaetano de Sanctis, de Viti de Marco, Levi Civita, Lionello Venturi, Guido de Ruggiero, Levi della Vida, and Francesco Ruffini.

Perhaps there have been other oath-requiring regimes which are of less bad odor in American nostrils than Hitler's and Mussolini's. Even if some should be discovered, however, such existence will not invalidate the actuality that both the Nazis and the Fascists required oaths of professors, and without—to put the matter mildly—any demonstrably good effect upon higher education in Germany and Italy.

A glance into the past reveals that universities were

having trouble with oaths clear back to the Middle Ages. In the thirteenth and fourteenth centuries there developed, for both professors and students, a great multiplicity of oaths. Curiously, the professors seemed to have confidence in oaths and demanded them of their students, who were made to take an oath of obedience to practically every university regulation. Some of these oaths sound, from the professor's point of view, like rather good ideas. Thus in some universities a candidate who was coming up for an examination had to swear that, if he was failed, he would not wreak his vengeance on the examiner with knife or dagger. On second thought, however, you will notice two weaknesses in this oath. First, it might put ideas in the student's head. Second, if a student was angry enough to go after the examiner with a knife, he would probably not be in a state of mind to remember any oath he had taken.

And as a matter of fact, the whole procedure of oath taking fell into disrepute. It simply did not work. In the end the professors discovered that it was better to find out who had broken a regulation and fine him. The immediate loss of half-a-crown worked better for keeping a student well behaved than did the assurance that for breaking his oath he would spend an indefinite number of extra years in purgatory.

Yet this idea of conducting a university by the oath technique is too attractive for us to pass it quickly by. In those days, instead of taking class roll, you had your students swear at the end of the course that they had attended the lectures; instead of making out an examination and giving it and grading it, you had your students swear that they had read the books they were supposed to read. (All this would certainly save the professor a lot of trouble.) Around 1350 anyone receiving the M.A. degree at the University of Paris had to swear about forty oaths, as to having done certain things (which probably he hadn't done) and as to being ready to do others (which he probably hadn't much intention of doing). Of course the administering of forty oaths would be a lot of work, especially if each one had to be notarized. But perhaps we could have the whole class swear in unison, or else, with modern efficiency, we might get everything into one big oath.

Yes, if some of our regents think so highly of swearing, we might consider going along with them and really get the oath technique to work again in the university system. Both professors and students might approve of getting rid of the troublesome two-week final-examination period. All we would need to do would be to concentrate a great and highly impressive lot of oath swearing on Commencement Day. The students who had attended their classes, read the books, and handed the assignments in would so swear; those who had not done so would of course be unable to sign their oaths. Then the signers would get their diplomas and the non-signers would be dismissed.

In some way, apparently, we have slipped out of the serious and even tragic mood in which this chapter was begun—that of imposition of oaths against a background of rising totalitarian aggression and the echoing tread of private armies. To make amends, let us now return to a matter which is, we fear, only too serious. Its connection with the general topic of this chapter is perhaps not quite so obvious but should offer no great difficulties to an alert and penetrating mind.

MR. GIANNINI AND HIS VIGILANTES

At the meeting of the Board of Regents on April 21, 1950, during the course of his remarks, Regent L. M. Giannini spoke as follows: "I want to organize 20th Century vigilantes, who will unearth Communists and Communism in all their sordid aspects, and I will, if necessary."

For the benefit of non-Californians, we should identify Regent L. M. Giannini as the son of Regent A. P. Giannini, who enriched the University with many benefactions. On the death of the father, the son was appointed to fill the vacancy on the Board. The son also succeeded to the rule of the financial empire built up by the father and to the presidency of the Bank of America, commonly known as the largest bank in the world.

The actual quotation as printed above is drawn from the San Francisco *Chronicle* of April 22, 1950. Mr. Giannini has not asked for a correction.

The present writer was in attendance at that meeting of the Board, which was an open one, and he can testify both as to the words themselves and as to the manner of their utterance. They were spoken with all the intonation suggesting deep sincerity, conviction, and determination. There was in the speaker's voice nothing to suggest irony or joking.

At the meeting I was sitting between a young professor on my left hand and on my right a young woman who was apparently a reporter for an undergraduate newspaper. The words struck the three of us with almost physical shock. We reacted with a sudden stirring in our chairs. The young woman recovered and began to scribble on her pad. She muttered something, but I caught only the unbelieving tone, not the words.

It was incredible! Here was a man voting to require from professors the oath that they were not Communists. In its original form this oath had required the special abjuration of any belief in "the overthrow of the United States Government by force or violence." Yet here this same man was declaring himself as ready "to organize 20th Century vigilantes."

As to whether Regent Giannini used the word "vigilantes" in any special or unusual sense, I cannot say. It is, however, a fairly common word, and we should all be familiar with its accepted meaning. Webster's New International Dictionary defines a vigilante as "a member of a vigilance committee," and a vigilance committee as "a volunteer committee of citizens for the oversight and protection of any interest, esp. one organized to suppress and punish crime summarily, as when the processes of law appear inadequate."

When Regent Giannini, presumably believing that the law enforcement in the United States and in California was inadequate, thus seemingly stated that he was about to take the law into his own hands, what reaction came from the Board of Regents? I was not well seated so as to observe the expressions of their faces, and I am not clairvoyant enough to know what occurred within their minds. But not one of them spoke in challenge or protest.

No elder statesman said, gently but reprovingly, giving a chance to withdraw: "But surely, Mr. Giannini, you cannot have meant exactly what you said. You perhaps spoke hastily. . . ."

And no younger man cried out in righteous anger: "What is this? You are advocating the opposite of the oath that you are requiring!"

No, they waited politely until he had finished speaking and had fully expressed his intention of resigning from the Board because it did not take a more vigorous stand against the professors. Then they urged him to remain one of them!

Not all, indeed! Some of them remained quiet, and we cannot know just what they were thinking, although they certainly took no positive action. But several regents pleaded with him to reconsider. They protested their friendship to him and extolled his personality, his wisdom, and his services to the University.

I tremble to think of what would have happened to a professor if he had risen in a meeting of the Senate to suggest a recourse to vigilantism. Certainly he would have been challenged and shouted down by his colleagues. Word of his action would have been carried to the regents, and he might have been summarily dismissed.

Moreover, there at the meeting I found myself interested to hear several regents defending the right of minorities. I cannot remember the exact words, but they were in effect: "Mr. Giannini, you should not resign because you are a minority" . . . "We respect the rights of minorities" . . . "Each of us has, in his time, been in a minority on this Board." Even that regent who had most severely castigated the "dissident minority" on the faculty was loud in his praise of the independence of spirit shown by Mr. Giannini's dissidence. Perhaps I should be ashamed of such mean thoughts, but I cannot help thinking: "There seems to be a difference between a minority composed of many scores of professors and a minority composed of the president of the Bank of America."

Since the implication of Regent Giannini's statement, if taken in its obvious sense, is so terrible, one tries to think of ways in which his words can be charitably interpreted.

Should they be considered the outpourings of an immature personality, under the influence of pent-up anger, speaking with the latitude allowed a rich man?

Or should they be thought as the words of a banker panicky about the rights of property? On that same occasion he also said: "I think everyone is underestimating the Communist threat to our whole economy," and his use of "economy" rather than "way of life" or "democracy" may be significant.

Or should his statement be considered as merely that of a man not gifted in language who did not realize what his words meant?

Or, on the other hand, is he a man too prone to flights of imagination, even to poetry, as when he said on that same occasion: "I feel sincerely that if we rescind this oath flags will fly from the Kremlin"?

But even if we accept any of these more charitable interpretations, why did his colleagues not challenge what he had said? They were, to be sure, worn down with the long struggle; and, as with the faculty, a kind of apathy had probably begun to take hold of them. We may charitably assume that they were tired. Yet Mr. Giannini's words, if the dictionary interpretation of the words be accepted, had expressed an intention and announced a private plan for the organization of vigilantes, for taking the law into his own hands. I cannot believe that such plans are approved by the other members of the Board. But, if not approved, are they such plans as the other members of the Board feel not much objection to—not enough to make it worth while to commit the impropriety of speaking up impolitely?

I would not imply that the other twenty regents present should be held guilty by association, but I think that they might have spoken.

And as I think back I also might have spoken. To my own shame I did not rise up and cry out. I would probably have been immediately ejected from the meeting, and perhaps from my professorship in due course. Still, it would have been a fine thing to remember!

Here, as I write, I am trying to act in expiation—to make amends for my slow thinking, or my cowardice, at that moment.

Perhaps all this is of no importance now that Mr. Giannini has resigned. Perhaps I should say nothing, even by implication, against "the good regents." Still, a book of considerable antiquity and repute declares, "To every thing there is a season . . . a time to keep silence, and a time to speak." This is not—I believe—a time nor an occasion to keep silence.

Part Four: The Regential System

CHAPTER 11

Memory Book

In a statement to the press on February 28, 1950, Regent John Francis Neylan declared:

In the relatively short life of 81 years, under the guidance of the regents, the university has achieved a position of eminence seldom equaled in the United States or elsewhere.

Academic freedom has been guarded zealously and jealously. (San Francisco Chronicle, *March 1, 1950.)*

We assume that Regent Neylan made this statement in good faith, and we wish that we could agree with him, even as regards that period of eighty years preceding the oath controversy. We fear, however, that he has not pondered over the pages of our two University histories.

Is it possible that Regent Neylan has never read or heard tell of the troubles endured by Presidents Durant, Gilman, and Le Conte?

Or is he wholly ignorant of the famous "visitation committee" sent by the regents in 1881? The faculty members dismissed in that year are doubtless long since dead, but their ghosts might well be called upon to pass in succession like those before King Richard.

Has Regent Neylan been so busy with other duties that he has neglected to read an interesting article by Dr. Herman A. Spindt, "The Dark Days under President W. T. Reid," in our alumni magazine, the *California Monthly*, for October 1949? On his resignation President Reid wrote to Regent D. O. Mills:

It will be enough for me to say that the Regents have so encroached upon the province of the Faculty and have so hedged the President about with restrictions as to make it impossible for him to carry out a vigorous individual policy.

President Reid ended his care-ridden administration in 1885. That is a long time ago, but it certainly reduces from eighty-one to sixty-five that supposed period of Regent Neylan's in which the University's Academic Freedom was unperturbed by regential interference.

That period would undoubtedly be still further reduced if we could get at the facts behind the bitter warfare between regents and faculty in the early nineties.

With the advent of President Wheeler in 1899, things became better. Wheeler was a strong president and kept his regents under control. The University grew to be, for the first time, an important national institution.

Around 1920, after Wheeler's retirement, however, more troubles occurred. This is still known in faculty circles as "the Revolution." Unfortunately, no history was written at the time, and the older professors still consider their lips to be sealed as to what really happened.

Under the administration of President Campbell (1923–1930) and under that of President Sproul until 1949, the record of the Board of Regents seems to have been excellent.

Unfortunately, however, what happened was that the long period of calm only allowed the forces of the storm to build up more tensely. During this period almost of a generation, while the University moved steadily forward until it occupied one of the first positions in the world, we of the faculty busied ourselves with teaching and research, considering Academic Freedom to be secure. An appointment on the Committee on Privilege and Tenure came to be a sinecure. The local chapter of the American Association of University

Professors gained very few members and developed much of the psychology of a "company union." When we heard of troubles at Texas or some other state university, we said complacently, "It can't happen here!" and went on to the library or the laboratory.

` Nevertheless, even in the long period of calm from 1923 to 1949, enough wind was blowing to move an occasional straw. The trouble was not with the Board as a whole but with individual regents. Various professors at various times suffered when individual regents interfered. In general, these cases cannot be presented, because the involved faculty members fear retaliation, especially in the present very disturbed state of affairs. We are fortunate, however, in being able to present the private war of Professor Bopp with Regent Calef. Since both names and details are well concealed, we hope that the narration of this incident will cause no embarrassment to either of the principals. We here attack the abuses of the regential system, not any individual regent. Besides, we are authorized to quote Professor Bopp: "The way things are now, I don't care much—as much as I used to—whether I stay at the University of California or not."

MY PRIVATE WAR WITH REGENT CALEF

This account of the oath controversy, they tell me, needs a little lightening. Well, here goes! Hear all about the slapstick shenanigans of Professor Elmer Bopp and Regent Ben Calef. Get ready to laugh. Only don't bother to unbutton your vest. It's not going to be that funny!

You understand that my name is not Elmer Bopp, and I say thank the Lord for that too! Also, I am not an ornithologist, and there is no such organization as the California Society of Bird and Lizard Watchers, and there is no such bird (so far as I know) as the white-footed titmouse. There is, however, such a bird as Ben Calef, though that is not his name either. The only real name is that of Bob Sproul, but since he comes off very well in this whole affair, I see no reason for changing that one.

It all began when the department secretary left a note for me: "Professor Bopp: Please call the President's Office. They are trying to get in touch with you." All this happened, I should say, several years ago, and so in these reported conversations I am not necessarily supplying the exact words, but I am sure that the essential outline of facts is correct.

Well, I called the President's Office immediately, as a professor always does when he receives such a message. They connected me with Mrs. Groueber, although that is not her name either.

"Oh yes," she said, "I've been trying to get you, Professor Bopp. Regent Calef has just written to President Sproul. He wants you to come and talk to the Society of Bird and Lizard Watchers on the nesting habits of the white-footed titmouse at their October meeting. Regent Calef is president of the society."

Perhaps she did not say "wants you to." Perhaps it was a stronger statement. I am sure, however, that it was not one of the usual polite expressions, "would be happy if you would," . . . "would like you to."

I thought fast, and by long habit a professor is likely to be extremely respectful and obliging when he is dealing with the president and particularly when a regent stands in the background, if you could even call this "background." Then I sparred for time.

"I'm very busy," I said. "That means a five-hundred-mile trip. I hardly think that I can take the time this fall."

There was a pause at the other end of the line, and I took it as indicating a certain dramatization of shock.

"But," she said, "Regent Calef has written a letter!"

At that moment I had an image of Bop Sproul as the keeper of a livery stable and of all the professors as livery horses and of Regent Calef ordering out a horse for his own purposes.

"Well, I'm sorry," I said, "but as I think things over, I find that I really am too busy to take most of two days for that purpose. Will you please tell President Sproul that I'm sorry and ask him to express my appreciation to Regent Calef that he thought I would make a good speech?"

I supposed that the matter had ended there. I get a fair number of invitations to speak. Since I really am busy, I turn down nearly all of them, particularly when they make no mention of honorarium or even of traveling expenses. I didn't for a moment consider that Bob Sproul would hold the matter against me, and as for Regent Calef, I figured that he was so far away, academically speaking, that any resentment he might feel would have no very good route by which to express itself.

Within two hours I had another call from the President's Office. This time it was the president himself. "HELLO, ELMER," he said.

"Hello, Bob," I said in reply.

"About this speech to the Bird and Lizard Watchers," he said, "Calef would really like to have you do that. He thinks that you're the best possible man for the topic."

"Well, that's very complimentary of him. Possibly I am. Of course it's a long time since I did that monograph on the titmouse, and I really haven't much interest in the topic any more."

"Yes, I'd say that you'd gone on to higher and bigger things. But still, you could make the talk."

"Naturally I can't say that I couldn't make it. But, as I told Mrs. Groueber, I'm very busy just now, and I've turned down various invitations to speak."

"I know," he said, "I realize that. Still, this would be a service. This would be a personal favor to me."

Bob Sproul has been a good friend to me and he has a lot of charm too. When he spoke of a personal favor, I felt myself weakening fast. Then the image of the livery stable came into my mind.

"All right, Bob," I said, "I might as well tell you. Of course I could squeeze out the time somewhere, but what I really object to is being ordered out like a livery-stable horse by means of a letter that a regent writes to the president."

There was a pause on the line again.

"All right," he said then, "I think I understand. I'll take care of it. It won't be easy, but I'll take care of it."

He hung up, and I hung up. I thought again that the matter was finished.

Next day I had a third call from the President's Office. It was the president himself again.

"I've talked with Calef on the telephone," he said. "He really is very much worked up about having you come to speak."

I'm afraid that I can be just as stubborn as the next one. Anyway, I'd gone too far, I felt, to back down.

"I'm sorry, and I mean it, Bob. I'd like to help you out here. But I took my position really as a moral issue, and I don't see how I can back down."

"Well, I wish you could! With things as they are, this would be a University service. It would make my job easier."

I was really beginning to feel like a heel now, letting the University down, and Bob too. Still, it would be worse to yield now than it would have been in the first place. I thought fast for still another time and checked the sudden emotional impulse to be a good fellow.

"Look here, Bob. How about this? Why doesn't Mr. Calef write me a letter on their stationery as president of the society, not as a regent? In that case I'll consider it."

This didn't seem to please him. I gathered that Calef wasn't likely to back down any more than I was and that such a situation left Bob Sproul badly caught in between.

"I'm sorry!" I said once more. "This probably leaves you in a bad fix."

"Oh, don't worry about me! I'm used to that!" He seemed a little pathetic.

"Well," I said, perhaps nervously defensive, "I'd think you'd like having a good, vigorous, independent-minded faculty that doesn't like to take orders."

"Yes," he said, "I do." But he didn't seem very enthusiastic, and I can't say that at the moment I blamed him. And again I thought the matter was all over.

Two or three days later, at my home, I received a letter, and the envelope bore the return address of the California Society of Bird and Lizard Watchers. It contained a polite letter requesting that I speak, etc., etc. It was signed Ben Calef, and underneath the signature was typewritten, "President of the Society."

There I was, caught in my own trap! I really didn't want to make that trip and to talk to that society—let alone on that subject. But I had to write to Mr. Ben Calef, President of the Society, and accept. His letter had made no statement as to compensation. I think, however, that it is indecent for a man to pay his own expenses to make a speech. I therefore inserted the sentence that I would expect my expenses. . . .

So I went and I made my speech. Mr. Calef, incidentally, was not there. They told me that he was out of town. People came up and complimented me after I had finished. I don't think, however, that it was a very good speech. The way I had got into making it did not arouse much enthusiasm in me.

When I was about to leave, the secretary spoke to me and said that President Calef—or she may have said Regent Calef—would take care of my expenses if I would submit a bill. I thanked her.

I spent that night with a friend and ate breakfast at his house. When I got back home I sent in a bill for expenses, which consisted exactly of my round-trip airplane fare—$42.50.

I waited a month. Then I got another call from the President's Office, and it was Bob Sproul again.

"Say, Elmer," he said, "Calef has sent me the bill for those expenses on your trip to speak to his society. It's only for $42.50. That's not very much. Was that all the expense you had?"

I was flabbergasted at just how the bill had got to him, but I answered his question first:

"That's all the bill I sent in. I stayed with a friend. I just sent the bill for my airplane ticket."

"Well, if that's all you think is right——"

"No, I don't want to charge anything more. As you remember, my heart wasn't in that affair. I'm afraid I didn't make a very good speech."

"Well——" he said doubtfully. "If you only made them the $42.50 speech, I suppose that's all right not to get any more money than that."

"But how's it happen," I said, sensing my chance to get a word in, "how's it happen that Mr. Calef sent the bill to you?"

"Don't worry," he said, "I won't have to pay it out of my own pocket. There's a fund for these things. Calef just sent me the bill and said the University could pay it."

"I don't like it," I said. "Even if the University has a public relations fund for sending professors around the state to spread culture, I think the Club should pay the expenses, for they originated the idea."

He replied to the general effect that I might as well take the money and consider the affair finished. I was sure that that would be the easiest way for him, and I agreed.

I promptly got a check for $42.50, signed by the president personally. . . .

This is my own little affair, and I think that it has its comical sides, although before the end all the farce becomes pretty stale. And even in my little story there are some bits of seriousness. Perhaps they should be clear enough to anyone, but I am going to point them out anyway.

First—and this, I think, irritates me most of all—the president's time was taken up to a disproportionate and alarming degree because, apparently, a regent was involved. The president made three personal telephone calls to me. He called Calef at least once, perhaps oftener. He signed me a check personally. The president is very busy, chronically overworked. But just because a regent was involved, he had to expend all this time, not to mention what worry was involved!

Second—Regent Calef felt that he could incur expenses for

the benefit of a society of which he was president and then make the University foot the bill.

Third—Regent Calef seemed to feel that a professor is a livery horse so far as a regent is concerned and can be ordered out by the process of writing a letter to the stablekeeper. The matter involved here is not merely that the professor's own sense of worth and dignity is impaired, but also that no option is left either to the President or to the professor as to whether the professor's time can be expended better in that particular way or in some other for the greater benefit of the people of the state.

CHAPTER 12

Do the Regents Represent the People?

During the Year of the Oath many contributions to the letter columns of the press showed a certain idea to be very widespread: "The regents represent the people." Beginning thus, an argument proceeded in a manner disastrous to the faculty position. It may be summarized. (1) The regents represent the people. (2) Therefore, the regents represent democracy. (3) Therefore, the faculty represent an anti-democratic position. (4) Therefore, the faculty are Communists.

There is no need to attack the obvious logical fallacies of this argumentative chain—better to attack the original premise from which it starts. In so doing, we shall use the California situation, but the argument is applicable widely throughout the United States. . . .

The Board of Regents of the University of California consists of twenty-four members. Of these, eight are ex officio regents, each of whom holds his seat on the Board by virtue of his incumbency of some other office. This system was set up in 1868 and has since then been changed only by the addition of the president of the Alumni Association and the President of the University.

The original intention in setting up these ex officio regents was, apparently, to make them represent the people by insuring that certain elected state officials would sit on the

Board and that certain important groups within the state would be represented. Unfortunately, the particular structure is now long out of date, and the original intention is no longer fulfilled. Little else could be expected of something that was set up during the decade of the Civil War and has not been much changed since that time. In 1868 the Founding Fathers were doubtless justified, for instance, in establishing a representative for agriculture but not for labor or medicine. But we can scarcely defend such lopsided representation in the year 1950.

Let us run through the list of the *ex officio* regents, presenting them in their conventional order.

1. *The Governor.* He is elected by the people, and is also charged with the appointment of other regents. He is busy with many duties and ordinarily does not find time to meet with the Board. Nevertheless, the inclusion of the governor among the members of the Board seems natural and proper, a prerogative and responsibility of his supreme rank in the state.

2. *The Lieutenant Governor.* He has generally been a person of considerably smaller caliber than the governor. Although elected by the people, he is usually elected as a mere appendage of the governor, as the result of his nomination by a political machine. He usually has no special qualification as a regent, and being busy with other duties and normally more interested in politics than in higher education, he rarely attends meetings of the Board. The present incumbent is believed never to have attended a meeting until that of February 24, 1950, when he appeared, apparently in order to vote against the governor and the faculty position.[1]

3. *The Speaker of the Assembly.* Elected to the Assembly by the vote of his own district, the Speaker holds his special

---

[1] As scholars, we are humiliated at using such a vague expression as "is believed." Although public records, the minutes of the Regents' meetings are kept from the public by various devices. A well-wishing citizen employed a worker to try to obtain these records in order to check for this book the attendance of the

office and his seat as regent by virtue of being elected Speaker by the other assemblymen. His situation is in most respects analogous to that of the lieutenant governor. The present incumbent is believed never to have attended a meeting of the Board until February 24, 1950.

4. *The State Superintendent of Public Instruction.* Elected by the people, this official is inherently a valuable member of the Board because of his knowledge of the general educational situation throughout the state.

5. *The President of the State Board of Agriculture.* The Board is appointed by the governor, who also designates one of its members to serve as president. The chief argument against his inclusion among the regents is that by this procedure a vested representation is given to one field of activity, and at the same time representation is denied to other equally important fields.

6. *The President of the Mechanics Institute.* In 1868, and for some years later, the Mechanics Institute of San Francisco possessed the largest library in the state and was an important cultural institution. It now possesses a moderate-sized library, is a center for chess players, and operates for other purely local objectives.

---

various members and other matters. She did not even get past the secretary's secretary. We quote from her reminiscences:

"I was asked for what purpose and for what date or dates did I wish to see them. . . .

"The young woman with whom I had been talking then asked me to wait and retired to another office where a man was working at a desk. Presumably, this was the secretary of the regents.

"When she returned, she took me to the room where the records are kept and explained that the space was so limited that it would be impossible to give anyone room to work there and that the books absolutely could not be removed. . . .

"She told me that if my employer would write a letter to them specifically stating what information she wanted they would try to supply it if they thought the 'cause was a worthy one.' "

We scarcely need to point out the incongruity of a public agency being able to decide whether the "cause" investigating it is a "worthy one."

The Institute has fourteen Board members, seven elected each year. During a twenty-day period preceding the election of the Board, any member may nominate a member for the Board. To vote, the member must either attend the annual meeting for the election, or must place a ballot in person in the ballot box, open on that day only. Very few votes are cast by the more than five thousand members. It is usually very difficult to get a quorum of thirty at a meeting, and this is achieved, generally, by drafting the paid librarians and by persuading some of the chess players to leave their games for a few minutes. Once the Board is elected, it chooses its own officers, including the president. This regent, therefore, represents at most some thirty San Franciscans, and the situation resembles that of a "rotten borough."

7. *The President of the Alumni Association of the University of California.* Although seeming to represent a large body of citizens much interested in the well-being of the University, this regent is actually elected as follows. The executive manager of the Alumni Association, a paid employee, appoints a nominating committee. This committee nominates the president and the other officers. Any group of alumni securing a hundred or more member signatures on a petition may nominate a second ticket if they desire. So far as is known, this option has never been exercised. Lacking opponents, the official slate is declared elected. This seat on the Board of Regents is thus apparently in the pocket of the executive manager. In addition, the term of office as president is so short (only one year) that this member of the Board can scarcely become sufficiently familiar with its workings to cast an independent vote. Normally, moreover, several other regents are alumni, so that we may question whether a special representative is needed.

8. *The President of the University.* Although certain questions of theoretical propriety may be raised by having the president on a Board which is empowered to vote his dismissal, the inclusion of the president as a member with full voting power seems reasonable and meets with no opposition.

Of the ex officio regents as a group, one may naturally question whether most of them are likely to have or to develop any deep interest in the welfare of the University. The position of regent has been thrust upon them. If one of them develops an interest in the University, that is only a happy chance. Their attendance record at meetings is poor—particularly for those who hold political offices. But these regents seem ready to come running, like small boys to a fire, when a University issue becomes a burning political issue, as in the early months of 1950. . . .

As regards the appointive regents, the question might have been asked in 1868 whether the system was inherently a good one, likely to produce a fine board, or whether it would merely mean that the regents were to consist of the governor's political henchmen. Now that the system has been in operation for more than eighty years, we do not need to deal in speculation, but can merely examine what the system has produced. Has this appointive system produced good boards or regents, representative of the people in the proper fashion? To answer this question, we have compiled a complete roster of the more than one hundred regents appointed since 1868 and have made some biographical study, particularly as to the walks of life from which these regents have been drawn.

Have these regents been appointed for political reasons? This has apparently not been the case, at least in a grosser sense. The post of regent is simply not an important political office. In a fair number of cases undoubtedly the appointment has apparently been a reward for political services, particularly for campaign contributions. But an office which pays no salary and offers few opportunities for dispensing patronage does not appeal to the ordinary political heeler.

Politics aside, however, what sort of men and women (yes, three women) have served among the more than one hundred who have been appointed to the Board? Can they, as so many seem to think, be considered to represent the people of the state? Are they in any sense a cross section? Are they close in their thought to the ordinary citizen who pays his taxes to support the University and sends his son or daughter to be educated on one of its eight campuses?

Using Who's Who and similar sources, we have analyzed the professional records of the forty-one appointive regents who have served between 1920 and the beginning of the oath controversy. A similar compilation clear back to 1868 seems to smack too much of ancient history, but from a good sampling of earlier regents we find no reason to think that things in those early days were different.

The results (1920–49) are:

Lawyer	12	Clergyman	1
Business executive	9	Lecturer-author	1
Banker	7	Civic worker	1
Editor-publisher	3	Retired admiral	1
Physician	3	Clubwoman	1
Farmer	2		

The most striking fact of this compilation is the concentration in the first three classes. Moreover, these three might be considered an interlocking single group. Many who are here classified as business executives or bankers were trained as lawyers and often practiced for some time. All bankers are in a sense business executives, and most of them serve on boards of directors. Business executives certainly have close connections with banking. The three also constitute a single group in the sense that they are persons of importance in the business world.

Into this same large group fall also certain others of these regents who are listed under different heads. We doubt that either of the two "farmers" handled pitchforks and smelled of manure, at least in their later days. Both were operators of large enterprises in agriculture. One of them at the time of his death owned the largest lemon "ranch" in the world and was president or director, or both, of some fifteen corporations.

One of the three listed as an editor-publisher in Who's Who was mentioned in the Los Angeles *Times,* June 7, 1949, as "financier," and so far as is known did not raise any objection. At least one of the physicians also could claim the same classification. The clubwoman was a banker's wife.

The lawyer-executive-banker complex thus at the very least includes more than two thirds of the appointive regents since 1920, and in its wider implications includes *all of them except for a small and scattered group.*

This, we may add, is not a phenomenon peculiar to one state. Statistics presented in H. P. Beck's *Men Who Control Our Universities* (1947) show this same group constituting 71 per cent of boards of regents all over the country.

The classes of citizens totally lacking on the Board during this period are obvious but perhaps may be tabulated a little for emphasis. There was, during this whole period, no representative of organized labor, although the Secretary of the State Federation of Labor was appointed later, in March 1950—doubtless, to some extent, as a consequence of the oath controversy itself. During this whole period there has been on the Board no grass-roots farmer. There has been no small businessman, although doubtless some of these financiers started small. There has been no engineer.

Not wholly lacking, but strikingly deficient—in a body that guides a university and which therefore has a serious and delicate responsibility to the ideals of higher education—have been men of broad intellectual attainments in the letters, arts, and sciences. Of all people, they are the most likely to have a deep understanding of the nature and functions of a university. Men and women of this kind have certainly not been lacking in California, a region of strong intellectual and artistic ferment during the last thirty years. They have, however, barely had representation on the Board of Regents. . . .

All in all, we are thus left somewhat mystified at anyone's supposing that the Board of Regents represents the people. The ex officio regents either seem to represent very small groups of people or not to function effectively as regents. The appointive regents seem to resemble in their membership an expensive gentlemen's club. Legalistically, we presume, the regents may perhaps be said to be the people's representatives. Actually they come about as close to representing the people as does the Union League Club of San Francisco, an organization to which a considerable number of our regents have belonged. We consider the whole business too ridiculous to argue further. . . .

There is, however, another matter of importance. The real question is not whether the Board is composed of lawyers, bankers, and business executives, but whether such men are, as a class, fitted to dominate the Board. Moreover, even if we grant that every single one of them is individually a man fitted to be a regent—and certainly many of them have been, and are—still, is this very concentration to be desired? The question should not be primarily whether they represent the people well, but whether they serve the people well.

The usual answer is that men of this type are excellently fitted to handle the University's financial and legal affairs and that in those fields lies their primary business. Actually, however, the lawyers on the Board of Regents, no matter how able, do not handle the University's legal affairs. The regents permanently retain a law firm. Moreover, the regents need not be responsible for the University's investments; they can hire an investment counsel. We may also point out, or should hardly need to, that this whole book is evidence to the fact that the regents do not always confine their activities to legal and financial affairs.

Moreover, as has been often said, every man has the vices that spring from his virtues. A bold man will tend to be rash; a cautious man, to be timid. The same may be said, so to speak, of any profession. We need men of various kinds to balance one another. We might like, for instance, to have an engineer on the Board, but we might well view with suspicion a board on which there were a dozen engineers, and be afraid that a certain mechanistic philosophy might come to dominate the University. We might wish to see one man of letters on the Board, but tremble to think what would happen if it included a majority of novelists and poets.

The great concentration of wealthy businessmen on the

Board of Regents actually creates a gap between the regents on the one hand and the faculty and students and ordinary citizens on the other. In the University of California the average student is chronically hard-pressed financially. The average member of the faculty is well paid by the standards of his profession, but by the standards of the business world he lives in very modest, even meager, circumstances. The wide economic gap between the average regent on the one hand and the average professor or student on the other has created difficulties and will continue to do so. This problem is not peculiar to California; it exists throughout our public universities.

The amazing circumstance is that on the whole these boards of regents have functioned as well as they do. In routine matters and in quiet times they are at their best. Being to such a great extent, however, composed of men of similar professions, similar social status, and similarly functioning minds, they have an unfortunate tendency toward thinking mostly the same way in an emergency. They thus may lack the flexibility to adjust to a new situation. Variety in points of view is likely to be lacking. And a university is, unfortunately, a complicated and yet delicate organism to be built up only through long decades of carefully supervised growth, too easily wrecked within the space of a few months.

Such a time of crisis arose at the University of California during the Year of the Oath. During that time ten men nearly accomplished the wrecking of the University. In fact, even yet one can scarcely be sure that the word "nearly" can thus be written.

We may now do well to turn from the consideration of boards of regents in general, to take a close look at these ten men.

CHAPTER 13

To the Dissident Minority: A Letter

[*A letter conceived as written by the non-signers, jointly, to those ten regents who on March 31, 1950, voted to retain the "Sign-or-get-out" policy.*]

GENTLEMEN:

One of you was the coiner of the phrase "dissident minority," and in the press these two words have been directed against us as a term of opprobrium. Just why "dissident" should be coupled with "minority" we do not know. We would think that any minority in a controversy, merely by being such, would necessarily be dissident. What else, possibly, is such a minority but a dissident group?

We have, however, far more respect for the intelligence of the coiner of this phrase than to think that he used the word loosely or thoughtlessly. We conclude then that he used it, knowing that even a meaningless word, particularly if not well known to the public, can assume by iteration, especially in print, a sinister meaning. If this was his purpose, the maneuver was successful. The adjective "dissident," merely superfluous, came in the public mind to stand for something evil, and was thrown up against us as if it might have been "lecherous," "stupid," or "traitorous."

Well, you forged this weapon and, like most weapons, it can perhaps be turned against its makers.

Gentlemen, you yourselves are a minority, and therefore a "dissident minority." Out of twenty-four members of the Board of Regents you number ten. Moreover, even at the meeting where you voted together, you failed to constitute a majority, being equally voted against.

Or, to look at it still differently, compare your number— not even a baker's dozen—with our hundreds. Even if only non-signers of Senate rank are counted, we who never signed at all must number nearly three hundred. By the democratic test, therefore, you are put to shame, trying to enforce your will upon a group about thirty times as large.

You may, however, argue in your defense in two ways. First, you may say that by virtue of representing the people of the state you are a democratically preponderant group of millions against hundreds. This we refuse to admit. For, as we have just ventured to point out, your ten is not even a majority of the Board and so should, by any such argument, represent only a minority of the people of the state. Moreover, even the whole Board, selected as it is, does not seem to us representative of the people, and this has been so stated at greater length in the preceding chapter.

You may, however, urge a second argument, that even a democracy must speak through its leaders, that the ten on your side are better qualified to speak for the people of California than the hundreds on our side.

To answer this argument, it ill becomes us to speak highly of ourselves. We are merely a large group of professors, although we know that we have the backing of a large proportion of our colleagues. In the conduct of a university we may call ourselves not only professors but also professionals. Our average period of active teaching and research must be at least fifteen years. Almost every one of us holds advanced academic degrees, including the Ph.D. We could point out many among us who have gained high academic and professional honors, national and international. But let us go no further.

On your side, what can you ten present?

We have no wish to minimize your good qualities. Some of

you have served long and faithfully—and, in general, wisely —on the Board of Regents. That you ten are men of determination, not easily balked in your ends, not easily frightened, we—a little ruefully—admit.

We admit, also, that you have been, according to the standards of our time and place, highly "successful" men. With one or two exceptions you have not inherited the wealth which you now hold and the positions which you now occupy, but have won them by your own efforts. This ability to make and keep money which you have so well demonstrated, we are ready to grant, makes you superbly qualified to consider the University's financial problems.

But when you step across, as you have just been doing, into some other field, how does your case stand? Have you had great experience at teaching, thus being able to appreciate the problems of teacher and student, so essential in the work of a university? Have you yourselves conducted research, so that you know the difficult nature of the technical problems confronting the scholar and the scientist? Or are you in vaguer but still important ways qualified to be the leaders of a great university and to determine its basic policies? Perhaps you are deep thinkers, philosophers, penetrating students of the problems of civilization, so that we members of the faculty should humbly and gladly accept your leadership and take an oath out of mere deference to your opinion that it is advisable. Permit us briefly to examine your record and qualifications as a group.

We list you first by what might be called chief or principal occupation: lawyer (4), banker, newspaper publisher, architect, advertising man, osteopath, fruitgrower. In this listing we give you, here and there, the benefit of a doubt. One, or even two, of the lawyers might perhaps better be labeled "politician." (There is, to be sure, nothing libelous about this word, but still it is one which in our present civilization a careful man does not use lightly.) Moreover, the ranks of the lawyers might also be increased by adding to them the fruitgrower and the banker, both of whom have had legal training.

Some of you ten have at various times worked at other pro-

fessions that the one under which we list you. One of the lawyers was for a while a newspaperman. The publisher is listed in
one directory as "financier." In fact, we should be inclined to
think that nearly all of you would deserve this last classification, at least as a secondary one. Thus we find the fruitgrower
listed as a director of five companies and have newspaper clip-
pings indicating that the osteopath bought city property to
the value of $100,000 and that one of the lawyers sold his
interest in a gold mine for $325,000. Even the architect is
the head of a large firm.

Let us say quickly that we have all proper respect for the
occupations here listed and, like most professors, even stand
in considerable awe of the art of making money. Nevertheless,
we do not see how your training qualifies you, as a group, to
administer directly the affairs of a great university. Perhaps
the lawyers may have some conception of how a law school
should be conducted. Others of you may feel professionally
competent to judge in matters of the departments of Journal-
ism, Agriculture, and Business Administration. The University, however, conducts no School of Osteopathy, and an
osteopath is hardly competent to direct the affairs of one of
the country's finest medical schools. And even if we should
admit that he were, there would still be vast areas of knowledge unrepresented by the professional competency of your
dissident minority of ten.

Let us also look at your group with respect to its education.
(After all, you are attempting to manage an institution of
higher education.) Here is the summation of earned degrees:
A.B., 3; B.S., 1; B.L., 1; LL.B., 2; D.O., 1. Of these degrees,
the first three represent the minimal requirement of four
years. The Bachelor of Laws (LL.B.), in one of the two instances, represents graduate work done at an excellent school
after the attainment of the B.S. degree. The other holder of
the LL.B. lists no A.B. for himself, so that this degree probably cannot be considered an advanced one. The Doctor of
Osteopathy is of similar status. Only one of you, gentlemen,
carried on his work to the point of attaining any advanced
degree, and not one attained a Master's much less one of the

fully acknowledged doctorates, such as an M.D. or a Ph.D.

Three of you, indeed, fail to list, in our University catalogue, any college degree at all. Of these, one attended college
for a while; another attended a school of industrial arts; for
the third, we can find no record of higher education.

We are ready to admit, gentlemen of the dissident minority,
that a college degree may not mean very much. In fact, as
professors, we are in a position to know how little it sometimes means. We remember also that Abraham Lincoln never
went to college. But let us put it this way. Though your com-
parative lack of higher education does not *dis*qualify you for
conducting the affairs of a university, still it certainly cannot
be considered to qualify you positively for that high responsibility.

Do you, however, possess in high degree some of the less
professional but still very important qualifications for the direction of a university? Are you those deep thinkers, those
profound students of civilization that we have mentioned? Are
you men of outstanding eminence of character, of broad
cultural attainments? We have been unable to discover that
you are.

Only one of you, so far as we have determined, has been a
teacher, and he merely lists himself as a lecturer at a rather
undistinguished law school. As to authorship, one of you
records himself as the writer of a volume of boys' stories and
as a contributor to legal publications.

Perhaps our research has not been assiduous enough. Perhaps you have a whole galaxy of lights hidden under bushels.
But on the whole we doubt whether you possess such high intellectual stature as to qualify to be leaders of civilization, and
therefore of a university.

If our research has not led us astray, and if the composite
portrait of your group is at all a correct one, we should now
bring this letter to an end and sum up our conclusions.

Thus so obviously mere laymen and amateurs in the technical procedures of higher education and of research, thus so
manifestly not qualified by training and experience to think
penetratingly in any department of University affairs except

the financial, by what headstrong infatuation did you—a "dissident minority" of ten—think yourselves morally justified in enforcing your arbitrary will upon such a large part of a distinguished university faculty?

Eminently successful, we will allow, almost all of you have been in making money. Individuals among you are highly skilled in swaying juries, in manipulating sore muscles, in raising walnuts, in being elected to public office, in luring customers through the writing of advertisements. But in academic achievement, in experience as teachers, in scholarly and scientific attainments, and—as far as the record shows—in the longer and larger views of civilization, you are lacking.

As for loyalty, which in this controversy was—at least ostensibly—the matter at issue, we know nothing against your record, and we note that many of you have served in the armed forces of your country in time of war. On the other hand, we believe that the loyalty of our own group is equally above reproach. Moreover, we think that we, in as large proportion as you, have devotedly, in World War I or II or both, served our country.

Thus, as citizens, we hold our heads as high as you hold yours. As trained scholars, as professors at what we had, at least until recently, held to be a great and free and proud university, we believe ourselves much better qualified than you, in the present time of international crisis, to decide upon such delicate matters as the necessity or utility of oaths.

Most sincerely yours,

THE NON-SIGNERS

Part Five: Conclusion

CHAPTER 14

What Should We Do About It?

In a democracy, the university, like any other public agency, exists for the ultimate greatest good to the people. So much we may take as axiomatic.

The operation of a university for that end, however, presents many difficult problems. Few would advocate that the people themselves, by direct vote, should elect the president and the professors, or determine whether a Department of Finno-Ugrian Languages should be established, or award the contract for a new chemistry building. Experience also seems to show that the direction of a university's affairs cannot be well entrusted to the immediate charge of a legislature. Such elective bodies, their members chosen for short terms, have often shown themselves too readily and too violently swayed by the immediate political whim. The attempted solution of the problem of the direction of a state university has therefore usually been the setting up of a board of regents.

Whether appointed by the governor (as in most states), elected by the people (as in a few), or otherwise put into office, these regents are men, and occasionally women, of supposedly great integrity, background, and ability. They are charged with the high responsibility of directing the affairs of the university, through the intermediary means of a president and a faculty, for that ultimate greatest good of the people which we have already mentioned. Just how they should accomplish this end and adjust themselves to the president and the faculty are not questions answered in a sentence. Moreover, almost the whole of this book, beginning with its discussion of Academic Freedom, has been a demonstration of ways in which a board of regents may interfere with the best functioning of a university. When any system thus fails to work perfectly, anyone is privileged to question whether that system should be preserved. For the moment, therefore, we shall not even accept the existence of regents as being axiomatic or inevitable.

Actually, why should there be such a board at all? Is it a typically American custom of thinking in terms of business? Because our profit-making corporations are organized on the progression stockholders-directors-management-employees, do we therefore think that a university is necessarily organized people-regents-administration-faculty? Is the existence of these boards perhaps nothing more than a hangover from an era in which professors were notoriously impractical men, concerned chiefly with teaching such unworldly subjects as ancient Greek and theology? Now we have professors of accounting, of business administration, of finance, of city planning. Is not a modern faculty competent to conduct its own affairs, even its own financial affairs? Moreover, a modern faculty has many contacts with the affairs of the people, is drawn from many levels of society, and is certainly more representative of the general public than is the average board of regents. Also, by their necessarily close association with the students, the professors certainly keep more intimately in touch with the problems of youth than does the president of a bank or a partner in a large law firm.

This whole idea may be visionary. Granted, many strong arguments can be adduced against complete faculty control. Nevertheless, as between control by the average board of regents as now constituted and by the average faculty as now constituted, a case might be made in favor of the latter.

We are not, however, faced with this sharp alternative. There is much good in the regential system. Certainly we can find much to praise and much to preserve in the system under which the University, through nearly a century, has grown from nothing at all to one of the world's outstanding institutions of instruction and research. In considering the one group of ten, we should not forget the other group of ten who stood so stanchly on the side of Academic Freedom. We should remember also all those good regents who served in former decades. Even in the trying months of the Year of the Oath the regential system was far from proving itself wholly incapable of exercising· the high duties entrusted to it. Before advocating the abandonment of the system, or even the weakening of its power, we should see whether it may not be saved by reform. . . .

Like other parts of this work, the present section does not represent the ideas of any one man. From a collection and winnowing of opinions several positive proposals are put forward. This section may be considered to some extent the reverse of Chapter 12, in which the regential system was negatively criticized.

(1) A board should not be large. In some states a board with as few as seven members has been found satisfactory. Twenty-four members form too large a body, and as a result there is likely to be a low average attendance at meetings and too little individual responsibility. The number might advantageously be halved.

(2) The composite problem of age, length of appointment, and reappointment should be considered. A long-term appointment seems to be generally approved, so that the individual regents may be, like judges, removed from immediate pressures and so that no single governor will be likely to have the opportunity to appoint a majority of the Board. Whether the term need be as long as sixteen years, however, may be doubted. Twelve might be sufficient.

The long-term appointment certainly raises difficulties of age. Nearly everyone seems to agree that a board which is responsible for a university composed largely of a student body of young people should not itself have one foot in the grave. There is also the obvious argument that any board entrusted with great power for the public good should possess the full vigor of manhood and be more swayed by hope of the future than by recollection of the past.

Yet a really young person can rarely be appointed to the Board, and the usual appointee is well on in middle age. Before the end of his sixteen-year term he is likely to be approaching, or to have passed, the ordinary age of retirement. Moreover, the polite convention of reappointment has been built up, and before he can have completed thirty-two years as a regent, the average appointee will be far advanced toward death or incapacity.

Very long service is for other reasons also not likely to be wholly beneficial to the University. The history of the Board shows that a member who has served on it for many years is likely to become dictatorially powerful. Now and then we have seen the emergence of what has been termed a "boss regent," one who dominates the Board and begins to think that he individually runs the University, or even owns it.

Many ways may be suggested to keep the average age lower. The length of the term could be shortened. Reappointment might be forbidden or be made rarer in practice. Appointment or reappointment after a certain age might be forbidden. An actual age of retirement from the Board could be established, as at the University of Chicago. More possibilities can be suggested, but these and all others should naturally be considered in connection with other reforms.

This argument against extreme age must be maintained in spite of our full recollection that some of our best regents have continued to be such when they had long passed seventy. The exception must be granted to exist, but the exception should not be allowed to overthrow the law of averages for a regent any more than for a professor or anyone else.

(3) The archaic ex officio system should be radically altered. This is a peculiarly California problem but is not without its counterparts in other states. Of the present eight ex officio members, the consensus of opinion seems to be that only the governor, the president of the University, and per-

haps the superintendent of public instruction should be so continued. The arguments against the other ex officio seats on the Board are presented in Chapter 12. Since the Board is also held to be too large, the reduction of the number of ex officio regents would be doubly advantageous.

(4) The attempt should be made, either by constitutional amendment or by a change of traditional practices, to have a board more representative of the people of the state. If some such principle should be adopted, the agricultural representative might well be continued, and there would be added some others, such as an engineer, a scientist, a physician, a man of letters. The recent appointment of a labor representative has met with much approbation. Most certainly, moreover—and here faculty opinion is most strongly mobilized—there should be an academic representative.

Many have suggested that a member of the faculty, or more than one, perhaps elected by the Senate, should serve on the Board of Regents. The idea, however, meets with considerable opposition in the faculty ranks, chiefly because the man so serving would be placed in a most difficult position. He might, for instance, find himself forced, for conscientious reasons, to vote against some measure which a large majority of the faculty supported.

Nevertheless, the suggestion should not be passed over lightly. Particularly if more than one member of the faculty served on the Board, the position of each, individually, would be less difficult. Moreover, the term of service for such a member would presumably be much less than sixteen years; four years would seem to be long enough. And actually a professor serving as regent would not normally have nearly so much power over the lives of his colleagues as a professor now serving on the Budget Committee.

In the long run some faculty representation on the Board seems likely, for the simple reason that enterprises flourish better with co-operation than with jealous separation into rival sections.

At the present time, however, most of the faculty seem to

think in terms of academic representation, not from their own ranks, but by the appointment of professors from other institutions. The president of another institution might also be asked to serve, although many doubt whether the best faculty representation could be secured through an administrator. Regents also might well be appointed from the ranks of the emeritus professors. With the age of retirement now set at sixty-seven, a still vigorous and properly qualified emeritus professor might be appointed for a four or even eight-year term without exposing the Board of Regents to any unusual risk of senility. An academic regent, whether of emeritus or active status, would need no period of training. He would bring to the Board a knowledge of the University, more intimate than can ever be attained by a banker or lawyer.

Certainly, moreover, whether by law or by custom, at least two women should ordinarily serve on the Board. (Only three have been members in its whole history.) When the University student body is so largely composed of women, their absence from the Board of Regents, as at present, is indefensible. It is time that the Board of Regents ceased to be the state's most exclusive gentlemen's club.

Representation of different areas of the state has been a generally established practice, and as long as governors are politically minded, it is likely so to continue. It is a generally good custom, as long as it is not too arbitrarily prescribed. The governor should not be required to pass over an excellent candidate with statewide interests and appoint a mediocre person merely to represent some particular district.

The idea of representation, in general, should probably be invoked as a principle, not established tightly by law. Obviously one person will usually perform the function of multiple representation. Thus a woman might at the same time be a musician, an alumna, and a resident of the southern part of the state.

(5) By present practice, the governor merely appoints the members of the Board, without previous public discussion and without subsequent public review. The president of the Uni-

versity is indeed often consulted, and the governor can, of course, seek counsel from whomever he pleases to consult. He is not required, however, to make any public announcement that any particular person is under consideration for appointment, and the appointment, once made, is irrevocable. Friends of a governor and political allies to whom he is in debt—in past administrations even one or two rather shady friends and allies—have suddenly appeared upon the Board of Regents and had the right to walk in academic costume at the head of the Charter Day procession and to be clothed in all the dignity and power of regenthood.

Various remedies may be suggested. The governor might be required to call for nominations, and such nominations could be sent in by individuals or groups or by civic bodies such as the Commonwealth Club or the League of Women Voters. The governor might be required to make, a month before the date of appointment, a public announcement of the slate of candidates whom he was considering for appointment. This would give an opportunity for objection to be raised in the press or by other means, and the appointment of a really unsuitable candidate would be rendered much more difficult.

Finally, some agency might be designated for the ratification of the governor's appointments. Just as that interested body, the State Bar of California, is allowed to ratify certain appointments to judgeships, so—it has been boldly argued—that other interested body, the Academic Senate, might be allowed the ratification of the appointees to the Board of Regents. Such an arrangement might prevent the anomaly which occurred a few years ago, when the State Bar refused to ratify a certain appointee to a judgeship, although he was already serving on the Board of Regents, for which office no ratification was necessary. . . .

These suggestions are legalistic and institutional. Actually, of course, no board, no institution, can ever be better than the men who compose it. Under the worst system, some good men; under the best system, some far from good men, will be appointed to the Board. We can hope only for a system that will allow the highest average of good men.

No one, certainly not we who have worked in the preparation of this chapter, would expect the propositions here put forward to be quickly accepted, or the chapter itself to be made the immediate basis of a constitutional amendment. There should be a great deal more thought on the subject. There should be a much larger pooling of ideas. The minds of the regents themselves must be brought to bear upon the problem. In the long run, the regents should propose an amendment to the Constitution of the state, and this amendment, if endorsed by the faculty, would probably be wholly unopposed and would be adopted without difficulty. In the end, the regents should reform themselves.

CHAPTER 15

Unfinished Business

April 21, 1950, has been taken as our terminal date. On that date the regents voted to accept the alumni compromise and thereby rescinded the requirement of the special oath. To be sure, its essential words were transferred to the contract. Nevertheless, the oath as such disappeared, and therefore on that date the Year of the Oath may be said to have ended.

Anyone may naturally ask, "Who won?" That is a difficult question to answer, partly because the results are not yet fully known, partly because of mere problems of definition.

"Who," we may ask, "is 'who'?" In general one thinks of the controversy as being between the faculty on one hand and the regents on the other. We must remember, however, that some of the regents were on the faculty side and that the position taken by even a majority of the regents varied at different times.

The faculty also was generally divided and shifted its position from time to time, thus approving by a majority vote in March what it had earlier disapproved. A large part of the faculty, to be sure, consider that this reversal (the approval of Proposition ≯2) did not express the true opinion of the faculty, but was the result of economic pressure and the threat of dismissal, and so may be considered a vote taken under duress. Nevertheless, the vote stands.

The question, "Who won?" should perhaps be rephrased. Instead, we might ask, "Is the situation, as regards Academic Freedom, better or worse?" Or we might phrase it, "Is the University of California a freer and a better university than it was a year ago?"

The answer to such questions, we must dolefully conclude, can only be "No." The new contract, we must maintain, does not leave the signer as free as did the old contract. The objections regarding Academic Freedom (see Chapter 3) are probably as strong for the new contract as they were for the special oath. Moreover, the year has left a heritage of insecurity that cannot help affecting the individual. He knows that a teaching assistant was dismissed by fiat, without clear statement of charges or findings. He remembers the sheer tyrannical brutality of the "Sign-or-get-out" ultimatum, resting as it did more upon legal power than upon a moral position, and constituting an attack upon the principle of Tenure. We may therefore conclude that the cause of Academic Freedom has suffered a defeat.

The defeat, however, has not been a wholly disastrous one. The prestige of the faculty has suffered, and a few individuals may never be quite the same as they once were. So far, no member of the faculty has been dismissed, and the number of all those leaving the University is apparently not much greater than the normal annual turnover. A few are known to be looking for new positions, ostensibly because of the present situation—but it must be remembered that even in the best of times some members of any faculty are disgruntled, restless, or ambitious, and are looking for new posts. The personnel of the faculty is thus about the same as it was at the beginning of the controversy, and in some ways—having been thoroughly alerted and profoundly stirred—the faculty is actually stronger. The intensity of the struggle has died down, but a long period of adjustment between faculty and regents is probably beginning. The publication of this book may be taken as one point of evidence.[1]

[1] This chapter was written as of June 5. For the situation as of July 23, see Postscript.

As an indication of the way in which the faculty at least went down fighting, we may take the number of non-signers. Official figures have never been released for Senate members, but an unofficial poll taken by the Committee of Seven in April 1950 indicates that about 20 per cent of the Senate members had not signed the oath. In actual numbers this would mean about three hundred non-signers. Many of these, probably the great majority, would have signed under duress rather than be dismissed. Nevertheless, this is an impressive number of non-signers who went all through the year and still have their unsigned copies of the oath, suitable for framing.

The faculty retreat has not developed into a rout—and need not! Perhaps we should recall the expression "Pyrrhic victory." There have also been battles after which the retreat was begun not by the vanquished but by the victor.

In any case, we may point to three evidences of a not too crushing defeat, or of a partial faculty victory. (1) The oath, as oath, was rescinded. (2) The "Sign-or-get-out" ultimatum, with its automatic dismissal, was rescinded and by the same action the Senate's own Committee on Privilege and Tenure was recognized. (3) Regent Giannini, the die-hard opponent of the faculty point of view, accepted the result as a defeat and resigned.

In the larger sense, however, we should rather say, "Nobody won! Everybody lost!" Almost everyone will agree, for one reason or another, that the University is a less well-functioning institution, a less happy and creative place, than it was a year ago. The whole state has suffered in that the University is weaker and also because some of the publicity in connection with the controversy has been such as to make many people lose confidence, unnecessarily, in the University. We may even say that the world itself is a little worse off because of the year-long struggle.

Why did the faculty lose? Or, if you prefer, why did the faculty not win a more clear-cut victory? Looking back over the controversy, we would suggest that three chief factors contributed. (1) The whole controversy was carried on during the time of great national perturbation known as "the cold war." In short, the cause of Academic Freedom was too easily made to seem the cause of Communism, and in the hysteria of the time there was no opportunity to educate the public. (2) The regents, or whatever group of them cast the majority vote at any time, held the absolute legal power. It is always difficult for unarmed men to argue with men who hold guns. To legal power the faculty could only oppose moral suasion, a hint of obstructionism, and the threat of wholesale refusals to sign and resignations, which would have crippled the University but would actually have been much more disastrous to the faculty, individually, than to the regents. (3) The mere size of the faculty, though providing a certain moral force, was a handicap. This large group could only educate itself and establish its positions gradually. The reiterated charge that the Senate did not really know what it wanted was to some extent unfortunately justified. But could anyone reasonably expect fifteen hundred men and women—varying widely in age, in social background, in political and religious beliefs, organized into two parliamentary bodies—to come to a decision with the speed and clarity that can be expected of a single person or even of a small group? Moreover, the size of the faculty made its conduct of the fight difficult. The anti-faculty regents, it is reported, held a caucus on the morning of March 31 and then went to the meeting in full knowledge of their strategy. The Senate had to work at long distances and through committees. Moreover, it was not organized for action. There had been no real controversy with the regents for thirty years, and the Senate possessed no machinery for carrying on such a controversy efficiently. . . .

As to the future, what may we expect? If the present international situation continues, if Russia remains recalcitrant in the United Nations, if the United States is forced to move toward what is coming to be known as "the garrison state," if a defense of Academic Freedom can still be made to seem a support of the Kremlin—then obviously the future is dark, not only for the University of California, but for all our universities and for our traditional American freedoms. Such a contest, however, will be far too large to be fought out even on so spacious an area as that of all the eight campuses of the University of California. We of that faculty may serve as a spearhead and may supply some of the first martyrs, but we shall be only a small part of the struggle.

If we look forward to a future more in harmony with our American past, what may we expect? Even with this prospect there exists in the ranks of the faculty a good deal of pessimism. Some think that the regents, having won an initial victory, will press in all the harder and bring the faculty completely to heel.

Such pessimism, however, seems hardly to be warranted. In the first place, it assumes a certain diabolical quality, an intense drive for power, on the part of a majority of the regents, and there is little reason to believe that such a state of mind exists. Possibly a few regents, in the midst of the controversy, may have been so determined. But tempers cool. Moreover, there is every reason to believe that the individual regents— even those who most vigorously opposed the faculty—had their fill of fighting, were amazed and appalled, and before the end even frightened, at what they had stirred up. Anyone who attended the Davis meeting on April 21 could scarcely help sensing that the regents as a group, though they might still be determined, were extremely tired men. There was a dullness in voice tones, a droop to shoulders. In the words of an old American proverb, they had grabbed a bear by the tail. Even Regent Giannini admitted, at the time of his resignation, in words which we think we quote accurately: "We should never have started this!" By the very determination of its struggle, therefore, the faculty of the University of California, even if defeated, has probably done something to insure not only its own future but also the future of all the faculties of the country.

In addition, as we have pointed out, the faculty has been alerted and, to some extent, trained. For some time to come, we may be sure, the faculty will pay attention to the composition of the Board of Regents and to what the Board is doing. Even without legal power the faculty has, in the long run, many advantages. It is, for instance, composed of professionals, whereas the regents are laymen, not to say amateurs. During the oath controversy the faculty fought always upon the defensive, having allowed the regents to make the original proposal. In the contacts of professionals and laymen, however, this is somewhat unusual. Ordinarily we should expect the professionals to put forward the positive ideas. If the Senate, through the president, can take the initiative, it should be able thus to direct the future course of the University.

Moreover, the moral force of the faculty, though in an emergency it may seem weak, is very strong over the course of years. Not only is the faculty a much larger body than the regents, but also it is composed, proportionally, of much more distinguished individuals, at least from the University point of view.

Finally, the faculty possesses another enduring advantage. Perhaps someone may wish to argue the dictum, "The regents exist for the sake of the faculty." On the other hand, probably no one would wish to maintain, "The faculty exists for the sake of the regents." What this means, perhaps, is that one can conceive of a university without a board of regents but cannot conceive of a university without a faculty. And no one should forget that even during the just ended oath controversy a large number of regents supported the faculty stand. . . .

The many members of the University of California faculty who have worked upon this book pose an interesting question for the immediate future. Though their names are not here published, most of them have made no secret of their work, and nearly all of them could be discovered without much difficulty. They have sought for the truth. Having found what they believe to be the truth, they have expressed it boldly. They believe, moreover, that this expression has been in the best interests of the University and of Academic Freedom and American liberties. If the workers on this book are sought out and disciplined, or if retaliation is visited upon them in subtler ways, that in itself will be proof that Academic Freedom no longer exists in the University of California. . . .

At the end, let us address ourselves to our friends. . . .

First, we wish to thank the members of other faculties and all those others who have come to our support—by letter, by telegram, by editorial, by promise of support, by contribution of money. In these difficult times our ordeal is your ordeal, and you have recognized this.

We wish to thank also "the good regents." If at any point in this book we have seemed to include you among those who failed to support the cause of Academic Freedom, put it down to an infelicity of expression. Because of you we can still have trust in the regential system and in the future of the University. We believe that throughout the year you understood the situation and we think it only fitting to list here the names of Regents Fenston, Griffiths, Haggerty, Hansen, Heller, Simpson, Sproul, Steinhart, and Warren.

Another word—particularly to those young men and women who, having completed their professional training, now look forward to joining the faculty of a university. . . . If you wish, in the near future, a stable and secure post in which to teach and to carry on your research, we warn you that the University of California may not be such. On the other hand, if you wish to be in the forefront of the struggle for Academic Freedom, if you wish to be where much may have to be risked and much may perhaps be gained, then— if you can also accept the terms of our present contract—we call to your attention, not without pride, the still strong and distinguished faculty of the University of California.

Postscript (to July 23, 1950)

The compromise of April 21 established two routes of compliance with the Board's requirements; that is, (1) the signing of the contract, and (2) the submission of the individual to a hearing before the Committee on Privilege and Tenure, with subsequent review by the president and the Board.

In late May the committees, north and south, began to be busy with these hearings. Good faith on the part of the Board was assumed; that is, that only Communists, or, at most, extreme recalcitrants, would be dismissed. A discordant note, however, was sounded in the meeting of May 26, when Regent Neylan took the floor for twenty-five minutes in an attack upon the non-signers of the contract. This was widely interpreted as indicating his repudiation of the compromise. At this meeting the number of non-signers was announced as 412, of whom 94 were Senate members.

In spite of this speech the Committees of Seven, with what many considered to be unseemly haste and undue optimism, disbanded and returned $11,684.35, representing the balance of the faculty fund that had been subscribed.

At the regents' meeting of June 23, President Sproul presented a report based upon the reports of the Committee on Privilege and Tenure, and of other special committees appointed to provide hearings for many non-Senate academic employees and non-academic employees, and upon his own review of these reports. It was announced that sixty-two Senate members, not having signed the contract, had had hearings. (The discrepancy between this number and the previously announced ninety-four was not explained.) Action on the major parts of the report was put over until the next meeting, to allow the regents time to study the matter. Nevertheless, 157 employees were declared to be no longer in the employ of the University. Since all names were kept confidential, the composition of this group is, even yet, somewhat doubtful, except that they were all non-signers. No claim was made that any of these were Communists. None were Senate members, and apparently very few were academic employees. Many seem to have been secretaries, janitors, etc., who had neither signed nor applied for a hearing because of the simple fact that they were leaving the University as a matter of normal labor turnover.

With incredibly bad public relations, however, these facts were not made clear to the press, and headlines gave the impression, not easily corrected even by farther reading, that 157 professors had been found to be Communists and dismissed.

On June 25 the Korean war began.

The outbreak of hostilities against a Communist army, continued economic pressure, and the feeling that a small number of non-signers would have a better chance than a large number resulted in some signatures and resignations.

The showdown came at the meeting of July 22. In a small crowded room in a San Francisco office building, twenty regents met, with members of the Committee on Privilege and Tenure, other faculty members, representatives of the press, and some others. In a tense atmosphere attention was focused upon the thirty-nine non-signing Senate members who had had hearings, been "passed" by the committee, and been recommended for retention by the president. Regent Neylan, with his usual consummate skill, led the opposition. Regents Fenston, Haggerty, Hansen, and Warren spoke ably in support of the president and of the thirty-nine. One of these professors defended his position. Three members of the committee explained their work and asked that it be not disregarded by a repudiation of the compromise. As the moment for the vote was approaching, Regent Sprague, who had consistently voted anti-faculty, walked out of the room.

To take the vote, the secretary called the roll alphabetically. The first four votes were for disregard of the president and of the committee, and for dismissal. After Regent Pauley had said "No!" the vote was nine to six for dismissal. Then the last four votes came in as "Aye!"

This part of the president's report was thus carried, ten to nine. (Yes: Fenston, Haggerty, Hansen, Heller, Merchant, Nimitz, Simpson, Sproul, Steinhart, Warren. No: Ahlport, Canady [the new alumni president], Collins, Ehrman, Harrison, Jordan, Knight, Neylan, Pauley.) Regent Merchant shifted from opposition to the faculty in earlier votes, to their support. Regent Ehrman voted against the faculty in February, for the faculty in March, for the compromise in April, and in the June and July meetings supported Regent Neylan and voted for what the faculty generally considered the repudiation of the compromise.

After the result was announced, Regent Neylan shifted his vote to an affirmative and declared that he would move for reconsideration at the August meeting.

The rest of the president's report was passed unanimously.

The upholding of the committee and of the president and the retention of the thirty-nine (later increased to forty) should not obscure the fact that by the passage of the rest of the president's report six Senate members (and certain other employees) were dismissed. Although in the total picture the six are casualties of the whole oath controversy, the immediate responsibility for their dismissal rests with the Committee on Privilege and Tenure and the president. These six had appeared for hearings, but had not satisfied their committee. They were not shown to be Communists, and no such charges were even leveled against them in the regents' meeting. According to the chairman of the Committee on Privilege and Tenure, their fault was lack of co-operation required by the regents' resolution of April 21 (the compromise); that is, they would not make statements or answer questions, at least in such a way as to enable the committee to have positive and immediate evidence. Therefore, the committee reported that they had not complied with the regents' terms.

As to the justice and wisdom of the committee's decision upon these six there is individual difference of opinion. The committee members are of undoubted integrity, possessing intelligence and good will in as high degree as can be expected of human beings. They faced an extremely difficult situation, not of their own making. Certainly any adverse judgment on them should be suspended until they present, as it is to be hoped, a full report of their proceedings to the Senate. They deserve everyone's thanks for their arduous labors, which resulted in the retention of the forty Senate members. (The regents, who formally thanked the Alumni Committee, made no such gesture toward the Committee on Privilege and Tenure. Probably this was an oversight in the press of the meeting and will be later rectified.)

Since Regent Neylan is determined to move for reconsideration, and since the vote was only ten to nine, the whole struggle may not yet be ended. In any case, six Senate members—three of them having been on so-called permanent tenure—have been dismissed, and not for being Communists. The situation is not appreciably better, and is probably somewhat worse, than that of April 21, as summarized in Chapter 15.

Appendices

Documents

I. **Constitutional Oath** (Constitution of the State of California, Article 20, Section 3)

I do solemnly swear (or affirm, as the case may be) that I will support the Constitution of the United States and the Constitution of the State of California, and that I will faithfully discharge the duties of my office according to the best of my ability.

II. **Original Oath** (As passed by Regents, March 25, 1949)

I do not believe in and am not a member of nor do I support any party or organization that believes in, advocates or teaches the overthrow of the United States Government by force or violence.

III. **Revised Oath** (As passed by Regents, June 24, 1949)

(Constitutional oath, *plus* the following): that I am not a member of the Communist Party, or under any oath, or a party to any agreement, or under any commitment that is in conflict with my obligations under this oath.

IV. **Contract** (As passed by Regents, April 21, 1950, pertinent parts)

Having taken the constitutional oath of office required of public officials of the State of California, I hereby formally acknowledge my acceptance of the position and salary named, and also state that I am not a member of the Communist Party or any other organization which advocates the overthrow of the Government by force or violence, and that I have no commitments in conflict with my responsibilities with respect to impartial scholarship and free pursuit of truth. I understand that the foregoing statement is a condition of my employment and a consideration of payment of my salary.

V. University Regulation No. 5 (August 27, 1934; revised, June 15, 1944)

The function of the University is to seek and to transmit knowledge and to train students in the processes whereby truth is to be made known. To convert, or to make converts, is alien and hostile to this dispassionate duty. Where it becomes necessary, in performing this function of a university, to consider political, social, or sectarian movements, they are dissected and examined—not taught, and the conclusion left, with no tipping of the scales, to the logic of the facts.

The University is founded upon faith in intelligence and knowledge and it must defend their free operation. It must rely upon truth to combat error. Its obligation is to see that the conditions under which questions are examined are those which give play to intellect rather than to passion. Essentially the freedom of a university is the freedom of competent persons in the classroom. In order to protect this freedom, the University assumes the right to prevent exploitation of its prestige by unqualified persons or by those who would use it as a platform for propaganda. It therefore takes great care in the appointment of its teachers; it must take corresponding care with respect to others who wish to speak in its name.

The University respects personal belief as the private concern of the individual. It equally respects the constitutional rights of the citizen. It insists only that its members, as individuals and as citizens, shall likewise always respect—and not exploit, their University connection.

The University of California is the creature of the State and its loyalty to the State will never waver. It will not aid nor will it condone actions contrary to the laws of the State. Its high function —and its high privilege, the University will steadily continue to fulfill, serving the people by providing facilities for investigation and teaching free from domination by parties, sects, or selfish interests. The University expects the State, in return, and to its own great gain, to protect this indispensable freedom, a freedom like the freedom of the press, that is the heritage and the right of a free people.

VI.   The September 19–22, 1949, Resolutions of the Academic Senate

A. AS ADOPTED BY THE NORTHERN SECTION, SEPTEMBER 19.

(1) The faculties assembled in the Senate, Northern Section, wholeheartedly concur in the University policy as set forth in University Regulation Number 5 which prohibits the employment of persons whose commitments or obligations to any organization, Communist or other, prejudice impartial scholarship and the free pursuit of truth.

(2) The members of the Senate request the privilege of affirming their loyalty to the principles of free constitutional government, by subscribing voluntarily to the oath of loyalty sworn by officers of public trust in the State of California.

B. AS ADOPTED BY THE SOUTHERN SECTION, SEPTEMBER 22.

(1) The faculties assembled in the Senate, Southern Section, concur in University Regulation No. 5. They also believe that the University should prohibit employment of any person whose commitments or obligations, Communist or other, demonstrably prevent objective teaching and the free pursuit of truth.

(2) (Same as 2 above.)

VII.   The Adams Resolution, Section 2, a (As adopted by the Northern Section of the Academic Senate, November 17, 1949)

The Senate [Northern Section] approves the agreement between the Advisory Committees and the Board of Regents upon "the objectives of the University Policy excluding members of the Communist Party from employment" in this University, but emphasizes that it is the objectives of "impartial scholarship and the free pursuit of truth" which are being approved, not the specific policy barring employment to members of the Communist Party solely on the grounds of such membership.

VIII.

A. PROPOSITION ⚹1. (See Chapter 4 under dates March 7 and 22, 1950.)

(1) All members of the Senate will subscribe to the constitutional oath of loyalty sworn by officers of public trust in the State of

California, as prescribed in Article XX, Section 3, of the Constitution of the State of California.

(2) All future letters of acceptance of salary and position will contain a statement that the person concerned accepts such position subject to the University policies embodied in the Regents' resolutions of October 11, 1940, and June 24, 1949, excluding members of the Communist Party from employment in the University, and in University Regulation 5, endorsed in the Regents' statement of February 24, 1950.

B. PROPOSITION ✕2. (See, as above.)

No person whose commitments or obligations to any organization, Communist or other, prejudice[1] impartial scholarship and the free pursuit of truth will be employed by the University. Proved members of the Communist Party, by reason of such commitments to that party, are not acceptable as members of the faculty.

IX.   Three Letters, with Identification Omitted, Showing Divergent Faculty Points of View.

A. LETTER WRITTEN TO REGENT NEYLAN, READ INTO THE RECORDS OF THE REGENTS' MEETING OF MARCH 31, 1950.

I find it incomprehensible that some of my colleagues on the faculty consider it both an infringement of their rights and an insinuation of their disloyalty to be asked to take a special oath that they will protect their country.

These gentlemen are aloof from the practical affairs of life and from the alarm which millions of Americans now feel as to the designs of Soviet Russia.

Speaking . . . to Government groups, I have taken special oaths and been fingerprinted many times during the last three years. I have never considered that this indicated that I was especially suspect and I am astonished at the mental processes of my colleagues who do make such an interpretation.

I will sign a fresh oath daily, as I arise from my bed, that I will have no congress with Communism and will not thereby or in any other way destroy my country. Who would not take such an oath?

Finally, the claim that the responsibility of the university is

[1]The proposition of the Southern Section read "demonstrably prevent."

identical with the responsibility for the execution of our laws by the Governor of the state or a sheriff of a county is absurd.

I am astonished that my colleagues are willing to compare themselves in this way. The faculty of an institution of learning has a wholly unique relation to gifted youth, who assemble at their feet and can be indoctrinated, if not easily, at any rate, ultimately.

B. A STATEMENT FORWARDED TO PRESIDENT SPROUL, MARCH 6, 1950.

The Regents have declared war on the Faculty. They have issued an ultimatum, naming a definite date for compliance with their decree to sign a prescribed oath; the penalty for non-compliance by any employee of the University is summary dismissal, though he may have to his credit a distinguished record of service, and a reputation for unquestioned loyalty to the state and nation. No opportunity is to be afforded him to justify his refusal to sign which may be prompted by conscientious scruples and noble motives. In this respect, one accused of membership in the Communist Party is in a more privileged position: *he* at least is to have the advantage of "due process": *his* dismissal is to be decided upon only after definite charges are brought against him on evidence subject to investigation by the Committee on Privilege and Tenure. The contrast between automatic dismissal merely for refusing to sign and dismissal after judicial procedure in relation to evidence proving an alleged guilt by association, this is so glaring and ironical that a cynic might well draw the inference that in the eyes of a majority of the Regents the crime of opposing their fiat is greater than the crime of belonging to the Communist Party.

The action of the Regents is tragic. It is a declaration of war upon all those whose consciences cannot approve, and, who thus cannot accept as a condition of employment and tenure, a political test based upon guilt by association. Some of our scholars and teachers see in this test an invasion of academic freedom. To submit now to the fiat of the Regents, they rightly feel, is to open the way for later and more stringent conditions of employment and tenure, leading eventually to complete control of thought and expression. This suspicion is not unjustified in the light of the indefensible position of the Regents that all members of the faculty are suspect of being members of the Communist Party unless under oath they explicitly disavow affiliation with that Party. Suspicion begets suspicion. How is it possible to have implicit faith in the patriotism of the Regents while our own is so openly and insultingly impugned? . . .

The Regents may argue that in exercising their dictatorial power, they exercise it as an alleged right conferred upon them by the Constitution of the State of California. I hope the Supreme Court will find this right unconstitutional. It is an anomaly, to say the least, that in a democratic society a few men should hold such absolute power. By their action of February 24 the present Regents have shown that they cannot be entrusted with power so unlimited. . . .

Now I am deeply committed to the American Way of Life, and my loyalty to it is no secret. Loyalty to the United States cannot be extorted by threat or intimidation. The line between democracy and totalitarianism remains indelible so long as allegiance to the State or Nation is not exacted by external compulsion. The action of the Regents on February 24 constitutes, in my opinion, a denial of the very democracy we cherish and hold dear. It seeks to extract by force an expression of loyalty which is essentially un-American. America will not be saved by methods borrowed from Fascism and Communism.

My loyalty to my country is not for sale, and an extorted affirmation of it by the Regents is not the price I am willing to pay for my re-appointment. . . . I am willing, nay eager, to take the standard oath required of all public officials. . . .

My refusal to sign the prescribed oath, under the circumstances created by the Regents, is thus based on these grounds:

1. The oath is an affront to my dignity and integrity as a man and a scholar. The presumption that I belong to the Communist Party unless I specifically deny such presumption—this I find intolerable.

2. The oath is a limitation upon academic freedom. I cannot accept as a condition of tenure a political test implying the un-American doctrine of guilt by association.

3. I will not and cannot sign *any* statement under compulsion. What I regard as most revolting in the action of the Regents is their exercise of absolute power to force me into submission. I should be compelled to yield to force, naked and brutal, to ward off the threat of dismissal from the University.

This force can be met only by concerted disobedience. For my own part, I see no other course open to me if I am to retain my self-respect and respect for my calling.

I have served the University for thirty-five years, and have served it with all my heart and all my soul. If my reward for faithful service is to be summary dismissal, as a punishment for the crime of disobeying the arbitrary will of the Regents, let summary dismissal be my reward.

I will not sign the oath.

I will not submit to coercion.

C. A LETTER TO PRESIDENT SPROUL, MAY 12, 1950.

It is with deep regret that I have to write this letter of resignation from the University faculty. I had hoped this would never occur. My association with the University has been pleasant and, for me, a very enriching experience. . . .

I cannot accept the recent so-called "compromise" with the Regents, for, to me, it is a compromise with totalitarianism. And there can be no such compromise, be it communism, fascism, or any other form of totalitarianism. The latter is the main issue, not just communism alone. We all hate communism; we all believe in real living democracy. It is for these basic reasons that I must resign from the faculty of the University.

It is with complete sincerity that I realize the misguided people who introduced the "oath" hoped to effectively fight communism. It is my feeling that they adopted totalitarian methods by so doing. A "piece of paper" does not defeat an idea any more than does the killing of millions of men refute communism.

I also realize that those who have signed the "oath" or the contract (there seems so little difference) also hate communism as I do. The one thing that worries me is this: do those who have signed such a document realize they have *contributed* to the furtherance of totalitarianism? I recall the remark of the late Huey Long, "If Communism ever comes to this country it will come in the guise of anti-communism." While I pray this will not come true, I feel that those who have signed the "oath" and "contract" have capitulated to a form of totalitarianism. We all abhor this.

Is there no room for vision? Is there no room for conviction on things of this import? Can we not have the *courage* of those convictions? If we cannot, then I no longer wish to have what I consider a most distinguished position on a great faculty.

Therefore, President Sproul, as I said in the beginning, it is with real and very deep regret that I submit my resignation from the faculty of the University of California.

APPENDIX B

Roster

1. The Regents of the University of California. Ex officio: His Excellency, Earl Warren, Governor of California and President of the Regents; Goodwin J. Knight, Lieutenant Governor of California; Sam L. Collins, Speaker of the Assembly; Roy E. Simpson, State Superintendent of Public Instruction; Arthur J. McFadden, President of the State Board of Agriculture; William G. Merchant, President of the Mechanics Institute; William M. Hale, President of the Alumni Association; Robert Gordon Sproul, President of the University. Appointed: Edward Augustus Dickson, Mortimer Fleishhacker (term expired, March 1, 1950), John Francis Neylan, Charles Collins Teague (died, March 20, 1950), Sidney M. Ehrman, Amadeo P. Giannini (died June 3, 1949), Fred Moyer Jordan, Edwin W. Pauley, Brodie E. Ahlport, Edward H. Heller, Norman F. Sprague, Maurice E. Harrison, Victor R. Hansen, Farnham P. Griffiths, Earl J. Fenston, Chester W. Nimitz, Lawrence M. Giannini (appointed June 24, 1949, for remainder of his father's term; reappointed March 1, 1950; resigned April 21, 1950), Cornelius Haggerty (appointed March 23, 1950), Jesse H. Steinhart (appointed March 30, 1950).

II. Advisory Committees (1948–49). Northern Section: Joel H. Hildebrand (Ch.), Benjamin H. Lehman, Harry B. Walker. Southern Section: Martin R. Huberty (Ch.), Hugh Miller, John W. Olmstead.

III. Advisory Committees (1949–50). Northern Section: Benjamin H. Lehman (Ch.), William R. Dennes, Harry B. Walker. Southern

Section: Martin R. Huberty (Ch.), John W. Olmstead, Gordon S. Watkins.

IV. **Conference Committees.** Northern Section: Malcolm M. Davisson (Ch.), Robert A. Gordon, Joel H. Hildebrand, Wendell M. Stanley. Southern Section: J. A. C. Grant (Ch.), John W. Caughey, Martin R. Huberty, Robert V. Merrill.

V. **Special Committee of the Regents.** John Francis Neylan (Ch.), Victor R. Hansen, Fred Moyer Jordan, Sidney M. Ehrman, Earl J. Fenston, Robert Gordon Sproul.

VI. **Committee of Seven (Berkeley).** John D. Hicks (Ch.), Griffith C. Evans, Francis A. Jenkins, M. P. O'Brien, Stephen C. Pepper, Lesley B. Simpson, Raymond J. Sontag.

VII. **Committee of Seven (Los Angeles).** Paul A. Dodd (Ch.), Joseph A. Brandt, Cordell Durrell, Carl Epling, Neil H. Jacoby, E. L. Kinsey, Marion A. Wenger.

VIII. **Alumni Committee.** S. D. Bechtel (Ch.), Paul L. Davies, Milton H. Esberg, Jr., Kathryn K. Fletcher, Donald H. McLaughlin.

All authors' profits from this book are to be devoted to general faculty welfare.

Certain facts about the genesis of the book should be added to those already furnished in Chapter 1. Included in the group of workers have been members of the Academic Senate of all ranks from professor emeritus to instructor, non-Senate academic employees, non-academic employees, and "citizens generally." The group is a large one, even if we exclude those who contributed by sending in their questionnaires and granting interviews. At least seventy people must have helped in the work.

Although the original idea was to publish the book anonymously as a joint venture, more mature consideration yielded the decision that the book would be more authoritative if signed, and Professor Stewart was asked to do so, since he had originally conceived the book, had laid the general plans and organized the work, and had from the beginning assumed responsibility for the final form of the text. Although it cannot be said that every word of the book is his, he is at least in a position to assume full responsibility.

To some extent, however, the book represents the point of view of a group rather than of an individual.

Within the group working upon the book were individuals who differed considerably, one from another, in their opinions about the oath. There were probably no willing signers, but there were some die-hard non-signers, some non-signers of the contract, some who had signed the oath under pressure, and some who would have signed it under a "Sign, stay, and fight!" principle.

To indicate, however, that other points of view existed in the faculty, we print in Appendix A a few letters.

SOURCES

Because of the multiple authorship and because of the speed with which the work had to be done, there has not been absolute consistency in the handling of citations. Most of these are included in the text or as footnotes. The sources for certain chapters are here added.

Chapter 4 is based mainly upon official documents such as the reports of regents' meetings and of Senate meetings as given in the University of California *Faculty Bulletin,* together with official letters from the president, the agenda and minutes of the Senate, mimeographed reports of committees, etc. The newspaper files, particularly of the San Francisco *Chronicle,* have been useful.

Chapter 6. Material dealing with the Associated Farmers, including quotations, are from *Hearings before a subcommittee of the Committee on Education and Labor, U.S. Senate, 76 Cong., 3 sess., pursuant to S. Res. 266 (74th Cong.), Part 54.* The quotation, "Whether members of . . ." is from the Resolution of January 10, 1941, by Assemblyman Jesse Kellems. The quotation "Communism is not . . ." and the others in the same paragraph are from *Report of First Joint Fact-finding Comm. on Un-American Activities in California, 1942.*

In Chapter 10 the German materials are from E. Y. Hartshorne, Jr., *The German Universities and National Socialism* (1937). The Italian materials are from William Elwin, *Fascism at Work* (1934). The information on medieval oaths is derived from Hastings Rashdall, *The Universities of Europe in the Middle Ages* (1895).

In Chapters 11, 12, and 13 material was drawn from the histories of the University of California by William Carey Jones, and William Ferrier. We have also used the papers of Chester Rowell (Bancroft Library), the Constitution of the State of California, the Constitution of the Mechanics Institute, and the Constitution of the California Alumni Association. Biographical material has been drawn from Who's Who in America, Who's Who on the Pacific Coast, and from newspaper files.

For Chapter 14 we have found interesting comments on the regential system in H. P. Beck, *Men Who Control Our Universities;* Abraham Flexner, *Universities. American, English and German;* R. M. Hughes, *A Manual for Trustees of Colleges and Universities;* Alexander Meiklejohn, *Freedom and the College;* Thorstein Veblen, *The Higher Learning in America.* For a discussion advocating faculty representation on the Board, see Alan R. Thompson, "The Professor and the Governing Board," in *Bull. of the Amer. Assoc. of Univ. Professors,* v. 35, No. 4 (Winter, 1949). For a general discussion and synopsis of the whole controversy, see Dixon Wecter, "Commissars of Loyalty," in the *Saturday Review of Literature,* XXXIII, No. 19, May 13, 1950.